India's Green Startups

Entrepreneurs That Are Driving Growth

Jayant Sinha
and
Sandiip Bhammer

JUGGERNAUT BOOKS
C-I-128, First Floor, Sangam Vihar, Near Holi Chowk,
New Delhi 110080, India

First published by Juggernaut Books 2024

10 9 8 7 6 5 4 3 2 1

P-ISBN: 9789353458638
E-ISBN: 9789353453572

Typeset in Adobe Caslon Pro by R. Ajith Kumar, Noida

Printed at Replika Press Pvt. Ltd, India

Praise for the Book

'*India's Green Startups* is a rallying cry for action, spotlighting how India's visionary entrepreneurs are confronting the climate crisis with transformative solutions. This book showcases bold innovators harnessing technology to drive clean energy, sustainable mobility and climate resilience. This compelling narrative weaves data with real-world impact, proving that India's green revolution can inspire a global shift toward sustainability. A must-read for anyone committed to saving our planet.' – **Amitabh Kant**, India's Sherpa to the G20 and former CEO, NITI Aayog

'*India's Green Startups* spotlights visionary entrepreneurs that are essential if we are to tackle global challenges like climate change, clean energy and sustainable mobility. Jayant Sinha and Sandiip Bhammer reveal how these innovators are trying to build scalable solutions and cutting-edge technology, to position India as a leader in the global green economy.' – **Vinod Khosla**, Founder and Managing Director, Khosla Ventures

'*India's Green Startups* brilliantly captures the pulse of a new generation of entrepreneurs reshaping India's future. Their groundbreaking solutions are not only addressing climate challenges but are also setting global benchmarks for innovation and impact. This book is a testament to the transformative power of purpose-driven leadership in building a sustainable world.' – **Rajat Gupta**, Senior Partner Emeritus and Former Global Managing Director, McKinsey & Company

'As India's youth take charge, green startups are leading the way. *India's Green Startups* highlights the bold ideas and vision shaping a sustainable tomorrow.' – **M.S. Dhoni**, Former Captain of the Indian National Cricket Team and Chennai Super Kings, and prominent early-stage investor

'This book captures the remarkable journey of India's green startups, brought to life by Sandiip Bhammer and Jayant Sinha, showcasing their potential to transform the global climate narrative. Through dynamic and inspiring stories, it charts a path toward a greener, brighter tomorrow, making it a timely and essential read for anyone committed to a sustainable future.' – **Pawan Kant Munjal**, Chairman, Managing Director and CEO of Hero MotoCorp

'In a world grappling with climate challenges, *India's Green Startups* offers a beacon of hope. Jayant and Sandiip eloquently weave stories of resilience and ingenuity, presenting a roadmap for global sustainability driven by Indian entrepreneurship. An important read for leaders and changemakers alike.' – **Dr Soumitra Dutta**, Peter Moores Dean and Professor of Management, Saïd Business School, University of Oxford

'India's green startups tell inspiring stories of ambition, resilience and creativity, tackling pressing environmental challenges while building successful businesses. These journeys serve as powerful inspiration for anyone passionate about sustainability, whether they are aspiring entrepreneurs or venture capitalists seeking impactful investments.' – **Prof. Madan Pillutla**, Dean, Indian School of Business

'This book shines a spotlight on India's green pioneers, showcasing how bold innovation and relentless grit are redefining sustainability. It's a compelling narrative of local solutions with global implications – a must-read for anyone invested in the intersection of entrepreneurship, technology and environmental stewardship.' – **Prof. Tarun Khanna**, Jorge Paulo Lemann Professor, Harvard Business School; Director, Lakshmi Mittal & Family South Asia Institute, Harvard University

'India's green startups are not just businesses – they are bold ideas redefining how enterprises can emerge from a commitment to the well-being of society and sustainability, rising well above crony capitalism in their very essence. This book is a compelling read that introduces new perspectives on green business by Sandiip and Jayant.' – **Ritu Marya**, Editor-In-Chief, India and Asia Pacific, *Entrepreneur Magazine*

India's Green Startups

To Teddy, Aashir, Simran and Rishabh, and Punita with all my love and gratitude.

— JAYANT SINHA

To my father, Mahendra, and my daughter, Rhea - this book is a reflection of your unwavering love and guidance.

— SANDIIP BHAMMER

Contents

Foreword

The Green Tipping Point

India stands at a crucial moment, one that will determine not only its own economic destiny but also its role as a global leader in the battle against climate change. This book – *India's Green Startups: Entrepreneurs That Are Driving Growth* by Jayant Sinha and Sandiip Bhammer – arrives at this pivotal time. It captures the inspiring stories of visionary entrepreneurs who are redefining what it means to innovate, compete and thrive in a green economy.

The facts tell a stark story. Today, India is home to 1.4 billion people, yet it accounts for only 7 per cent of global greenhouse gas emissions. However, this figure is set to rise significantly as our economy continues to grow using fossil fuels. The stakes are enormous: continued reliance on fossil fuels could lock us into a high-cost, high-risk trajectory, while embracing green technologies could unleash a wave of innovation, job creation and sustainable growth.

Why is this shift so urgent? Consider our energy imports: India spends over $200 billion annually on fossil fuels, a figure that undermines our economic resilience and leaves us vulnerable to geopolitical shocks. At the same time, urban air pollution costs us lives and productivity, while extreme weather events devastate rural livelihoods. The path forward is clear: a transition to a low-carbon economy is not just an environmental necessity but an economic imperative.

As I reflect on the extraordinary entrepreneurial stories chronicled in this book, I am reminded of my own journey at Infosys. Back in the 1980s when we were just starting out, the idea of building global IT companies out of India seemed as improbable as it was ambitious. Yet, with a mix of perseverance, ingenuity and belief in the country's potential, we created an industry that put India on the global map.

This ethos of creating scalable, world-class solutions in the face of daunting challenges is precisely what animates the green startups featured in this book. They, too, are tackling issues of immense complexity – climate change, resource scarcity and environmental degradation –with solutions that are not just local but also global in their impact.

Jayant Sinha, one of the authors of this book, is someone I have had the privilege of knowing and working with for decades. Jayant has always been a well-known technology innovator, combining his deep understanding of real-world strategy with a remarkable ability to execute. Our collaboration began with Nasscom, where we worked on several strategic reports aimed at shaping the future of India's IT/BPO ecosystem. These reports provided the roadmap for how India could harness IT for economic and social transformation – a vision that has largely come to fruition.

Later, Jayant (when he was Minister of State in the Civil Aviation Ministry) and I teamed up on DigiYatra, an ambitious project that uses biometric technology to create seamless air travel experiences. Alongside the Civil Aviation Ministry, the Unique ID Authority of India (Aadhaar), India's airlines and airports and other partners, we designed a system that is secure, efficient and inclusive. DigiYatra reflects the same spirit of innovation and partnership that underpins the green startups profiled in this book.

Jayant's ability to see the big picture while diving into the details has always impressed me. Whether in technology, policy or now, sustainability, he has consistently been at the forefront of addressing India's most pressing challenges. His co-authorship of this book is yet another example of his commitment to fostering innovation for the greater good.

The entrepreneurs profiled in this book represent the best of what India has to offer. They are tackling challenges that span the entire spectrum of sustainability – clean energy, electric mobility, sustainable agriculture, waste management and beyond. What makes these startups remarkable is not just their technological prowess but also their ability to craft business models that align profitability with purpose.

Take, for example, BluSmart Mobility, which is electrifying ride-hailing in India while addressing chronic urban issues like air pollution and congestion. Or the pioneering efforts of Accacia, which uses AI to help real estate and infrastructure companies meet their net-zero goals. These startups are not merely solving problems; they are redefining entire industries, demonstrating that climate action and economic growth are not mutually exclusive.

The green startups featured in this book are following a blueprint that we saw emerge during the development of India Stack. India Stack revolutionized how digital public goods like Aadhaar, UPI and ONDC could be used to unlock new economic opportunities and deliver public services more efficiently. These initiatives demonstrate how collaborative ecosystems combining private sector innovation with government policy can deliver transformative results.

These lessons are highly relevant to the green transition. India's green startups are building their own stacks – of solar panels, electric batteries, biodegradable packaging and more – to create a foundation for sustainable growth. Just as UPI unlocked new economic possibilities, these innovations are unlocking the potential of a green economy.

Technology is a recurring theme in the stories featured in this book. Whether it's artificial intelligence (AI), Internet of Things (IoT) or biotechnology, these startups are leveraging cutting-edge tools to achieve breakthrough results. But technology alone is not enough. As I've often argued, the real power of innovation lies in combining technology with scalable business models and enabling policy environments.

Imagine an ecosystem where solar energy is seamlessly integrated with electric vehicles; where agricultural waste is converted into biofuel and where data-driven platforms optimize energy efficiency across industries. This vision is not far-fetched; the entrepreneurs in this book are already building it.

One of the most exciting aspects of India's green startup ecosystem is its potential to lead the Global South. Climate change is a shared challenge, but its impacts are disproportionately felt by developing countries. India's startups are uniquely positioned to offer solutions that are not only affordable but also scalable across similar geographies.

For instance, innovations in battery swapping and hydroponic agriculture can be exported to other countries in Asia, Africa and Latin America. These solutions, born out of necessity and ingenuity, have the potential to transform global value chains. As this book demonstrates, India is not just a participant in the global green economy; it is poised to be a leader.

While the stories in this book are inspiring, they also highlight the challenges that remain. Scaling green startups requires more than vision and tenacity; it requires an enabling ecosystem. Policymakers, investors and larger corporations all have a role to play in accelerating this transition.

Policy Support: The government must continue to create policies that incentivize green innovation, from subsidies for renewable energy to tax breaks for sustainable businesses. Initiatives like the National Green Hydrogen Mission are a step in the right direction, but more is needed to ensure widespread adoption.

Access to Capital: Green startups often require significant upfront investment, especially in sectors like energy and infrastructure. Impact investors and venture capitalists must step up to provide patient capital that balances financial returns with long-term sustainability goals.

Public–Private Partnerships: Collaboration between the public and private sectors can unlock synergies that neither can achieve alone. For example, government support for electronic vehicle (EV) charging infrastructure can complement private sector efforts to expand electric mobility.

Global Benchmarks: India's green startups must plug into global supply chains and supply the world's most demanding customers. To do so, they will have to ensure that their cost structures and technologies are among the best in the world. We have strived to do that in the highly competitive IT services industry. The green economy will require similar relentless focus on global competitiveness.

The green transformation is not just a challenge for entrepreneurs; it is a challenge for all of us. Consumers must adopt more sustainable habits, governments must set bold targets and businesses must reimagine their operations. The stakes are high, but the rewards are immense. As this book makes clear, India has the talent, the resources and the determination to lead the way.

In the words of Mahatma Gandhi, 'The future depends on what you do today.' The entrepreneurs featured in this book are taking this sentiment to heart, working tirelessly to build a future that is not only sustainable but also inclusive and prosperous. Their stories are a testament to the power of human ingenuity and the resilience of the human spirit.

India's Green Startups is more than just a book; it is a blueprint for action. It reminds us that the solutions to our most pressing challenges already exist – they just need to be scaled, supported and celebrated. I congratulate Jayant Sinha and Sandiip Bhammer for compiling this remarkable collection of stories. It is a timely and important contribution to the ongoing dialogue about India's role in the global green economy.

As you turn the pages of this book, I hope you are as inspired as I was by the ingenuity and determination of these entrepreneurs. They are not just building businesses; they are building a better India – and, in doing so, a better world.

Nandan Nilekani
Co-Founder and Chairman, Infosys and
Founding Chairman, UIDAI (Aadhaar)

Introduction

India's climate tech startups are driving the country towards a sustainable future. Green entrepreneurs are scaling up exciting new products and services for customers daily, reducing greenhouse gas emissions and solving many of the country's waste management problems. These entrepreneurs will generate millions of high-paying jobs, create trillions of dollars of new wealth and help India achieve sustainable prosperity. Their stories can shape your careers and their impact will define India's future.

Green entrepreneurs are creating several large, new green industries in India. If our startups achieve global leadership in these industries, they will become highly successful green unicorns. Some of these new green industries include battery swapping, hydroponic agriculture, solar rooftops, green fuels, waste management and recycling of waste materials, development of alternative proteins and fleet-based transportation services.

Net Zero is Net Positive!

We can only build a *viksit bharat* if we address the multi-dimensional impact of climate change triggered by global warming. Our planet has been steadily warming since we started using fossil fuels – such as coal, diesel, petrol and natural gas – on a large scale in the mid-1700s. Clever inventors in England discovered early on that coal – compressed remains of long-ago forests – burned with a high flame for long periods. These inventors began using coal to run large furnaces and steam locomotives in factories. By the late 1800s, coal-based furnaces drove steam turbines that generated electricity. This sparked the beginning of the Industrial Revolution, which laid the foundation for our modern, electrified economy.

Fossil fuels became even more important in the 1900s during the automotive age. These dense energy sources quickly found uses in transportation. The extraction, refining and distribution of fossil fuels soon led to the rise of major oil companies (such as Exxon and Shell) and oil-rich states (such as Saudi Arabia and Venezuela). The largest oil industry remains in the United States, the world's biggest producer of crude oil.

Crude oil also became a feedstock for plastics and other petrochemicals essential for modern life. Natural gas became vital for producing fertilizers for higher-yielding agriculture and generating electricity via gas turbines.

Fossil fuels power our modern conveniences – air conditioning, refrigerators, electrical appliances, computers, smartphones, cars and planes. But they come with a planetary-sized problem. When we burn fossil fuels, we combine the carbon in these fuels with oxygen from the atmosphere to make carbon dioxide (CO_2). Carbon dioxide is a colourless, odourless gas that gradually accumulates in the atmosphere. Before we started burning fossil fuels, the amount of CO_2 in the earth's atmosphere was about 100–150 parts per million (ppm). Today, it exceeds 400 ppm and continues to rise.*

The accumulation of CO_2 – one of the many greenhouse gases – prevents the sun's heat from escaping into space. Others are far more potent and devastating. For instance, methane is produced by the belching of cows and water accumulated in paddy fields. Agricultural waste also produces methane gas. Methane is also routinely emitted in gas fields through the continual flares that spew up from them. Methane is a hundred times more potent than carbon dioxide in trapping the sun's rays. Pollutants such as sulphur dioxide and nitrous oxide are other potent greenhouse gases. All these greenhouse gases are accumulating steadily in the atmosphere and warming our planet.

How much has the planet warmed? Data on average planetary temperatures has been carefully compiled by several top-notch scientific institutions worldwide concerning this

*'Climate Milestone: Earth's CO2 Level Passes 400 ppm | National Geographic Society'. *National Geographic*, tinyurl.com/2bh4mmcn.

question. They all show the same results. Compared to the pre-fossil fuel era (before industrialization kicked off in 1800s), global warming was slow at first, but is now increasing at an alarming rate. Between 1800 and 1950, the global average mean temperature on the planet only increased by about 0.5 degrees Celsius. Since 1950, the planet has warmed almost a full degree more, so that the average temperature is now 1.3 degrees Celsius more than it was in the pre-industrial era. As we pump more greenhouse gases into the atmosphere, the United Nations has predicted that the temperatures will rise by 3.1 degrees C by the year 2100.

Planet Earth is two-thirds ocean. So mind you, this is a 3.1-degrees increase in the global average mean temperature of our planet. Therefore, land temperatures may increase by well over 3 degrees on an average. These temperature increases become relevant when we start to consider the maximum summer temperatures we will have to face. For example, Delhi reaches 46–48 degrees in May and June. Climate scientists predict that over the next 20–40 years, maximum temperatures in Delhi could reach the mid-fifties! We could have heat waves lasting months with temperatures exceeding 50 degrees Celsius. In May 2024, the temperature in Delhi soared to its highest-ever level at 52.3 degrees Celsius.* These temperatures are likely to persist across all

*Kumar, Hari, and Mujib Mashal. '126 Degrees in India: New Delhi Sweats through Its Hottest Day Ever Recorded'. *The New York Times*, 29 May 2024, www.nytimes.com/2024/05/29/world/asia/india-delhi-hottest-day-ever.html.

of Northern India. Life without an air conditioner at these temperatures will become almost impossible.

As the planet gets warmer, other climate changes will follow. First, it will get much more humid because hot air can hold more water vapor. The sticky heat of July and August in India will become even more unbearable and it will feel like we are living in a sauna. Higher humidity also means that we will have more water in the clouds, leading to more intense cloudbursts, rainfall, flash floods and waterlogging.

Second, the Himalayan glaciers will melt faster, and this snow melt will lead to brimming rivers and flash floods in our hilly regions. There will be more soil erosion and landslides due to this fast water run-off. With more water in our Himalayan rivers and more intense rainfall, we will likely see much more flooding.

Third, the combination of heat waves and floods will dramatically impact our agriculture. It is likely that our rice, wheat, fruit and vegetable harvests will be disrupted. We are already seeing that apple orchards in Kashmir and Himachal Pradesh have been devastated by higher temperatures and apple production has fallen dramatically. Similarly, other crops may also be affected, leading to erratic food supplies and higher food prices in the country. Our growing population and agricultural sector are already under pressure, so our rural economy may be negatively impacted.

Fourth, we will likely see significant flooding in our coastal cities, such as Mumbai, Kochi and Kolkata. The Arctic and Antarctic ice sheets are melting fast as the planet warms up.

Icebergs are breaking off and then melting into the oceans. The net result is that ocean water levels are rising. Oceanic scientists believe India will likely see a 0.5–1 meter rise in sea levels. As this saltwater rises, our mangrove forests and marshes will be inundated and our coastal cities will have fewer buffers to absorb the seawater.

Finally, warmer temperatures mean more extreme weather events like cyclones and droughts. We will see more cyclones in the Bay of Bengal. Cyclones will also start appearing regularly in the Arabian Sea (which has much more open seas). Cyclones in the Arabian Sea have the potential to be much more destructive because there are many more large cities on India's western coast, such as Mumbai, Kochi and Goa. Cyclones can hit land with waves surging to 2–3 meters, causing massive damage to coastal real estate and infrastructure.

In sum, India must prepare for what climate change will inevitably bring in the next few decades. We need to first adapt to these changes by building a much more resilient economy. Then, we must dramatically reduce our use of fossil fuels so that we move to a net zero-carbon economy.

Many skeptics agree that we need to adapt to climate change, but they also argue that we should not have to reduce our use of fossil fuels. After all, the developed world puts greenhouse gases into the atmosphere by using cheap, abundant fossil fuels. Consequently, India has the right to use fossil fuels to power its growth and development. We should be able to emit as many greenhouse gases as we want. They contend this is the only fair way for the country to develop.

In our view, this argument fails on two important counts. If India keeps emitting greenhouse gases at its current rate, we will become a global pariah. Today, we contribute only 6–7 percent of global emissions, which is well below our global population share of 17 percent.* By 2050, at our current emissions rate, we will account for 20–30 per cent of the world's emissions. Almost all the developed economies are committed to getting to net-zero emissions of greenhouse gases by 2050. China has committed to getting to net zero by 2060. Our major trading partners, such as the US and Europe, may refuse to do business with us because we generate large quantities of greenhouse gases and put the planet at risk. This could have really damaging consequences for our exports, jobs and growth prospects.

More importantly, switching away from fossil fuels is good for our economy. Net-zero emissions are net positive for India! If we do not move away from fossil fuels and towards other energy sources, we will become a high-cost, non-competitive economy. Let's understand how this is happening. Massive Research and Development (R&D) investments and manufacturing capacities have been invested in core 'green' technologies such as solar power, battery storage, efficiency solutions and nuclear power. As a result, electricity generated from these new energy sources is cheaper than from base-load

---

*Deb, Kaushik, and Pranati Chestha Kohli. 'Assessing India's Ambitious Climate Commitments'. *Center on Global Energy Policy at Columbia University*, 8 December 2022, tinyurl.com/urx99b7t.

coal-fired thermal power. Electric vehicles (EVs) are cheaper to operate than fossil fuel vehicles. Factories that use electric-arc furnaces are more efficient than coal-fired ones.

Green technologies are even more cost-effective when the societal costs of coal mining, air pollution and energy security are considered. Note that we are not including the disaster-related costs associated with global climate change here. Even excluding the enormous damage caused by carbon emissions to the atmosphere, the destruction of forests and wildlife and the health costs of air pollution from fossil fuels, green technologies are far superior to conventional systems. Plus, we have to import almost all our fossil fuels from the Middle East, Russia and the United States. Our fossil fuel import bill is about $200 billion annually, accounting for almost quarter of all our imports! Reducing our consumption of fossil fuels is, therefore, crucial for national security and economic resilience.

Therefore, it is crystal clear that India should move to a green economy as quickly as possible. How will this happen? Who will accelerate our transition to a green economy? Where will the money come from? The answers lie with our outstanding green startups.

Startups to the Rescue

We believe India's teeming startup ecosystem will lead the way in greening India. Their innovative business models can enable us to switch our energy sources from fossil fuels to renewable energy. Through their efforts, all our electricity can come from zero-carbon solar, wind, hydro and nuclear generation. Green startups can get us to switch from petrol and diesel-fed vehicles to EVs. They can help develop game-changing technologies for steel, cement, fertilizer and other industries. Decarbonization is their business model.

Of course, the government (at both the central and state levels) needs to develop supportive policies. But the real work has to be done by our entrepreneurial companies. We must switch to renewable power quickly, and new energy storage forms must be invented. Our buses and trucks need to be converted into EVs. Additionally, we must switch to using electric two, three and four-wheeler vehicles. This can only be done by us as private citizens and through the companies that do business in these industries. These tectonic changes will cost trillions of dollars. And this is our job, not the government's.

India is now an innovation-driven economy. *The India Stack* may be India's greatest innovation since its invention of zero. By linking digital identity with bank accounts and mobile numbers, we have created a unique set of scalable digital public goods. These include a national payment system ("UPI"), digital health services, highway tolling ("FASTag"), passenger identification systems ("DigiYatra") and e-commerce services ("ONDC"). India's entrepreneurs have eagerly built on these digital public goods to develop various innovative solutions, which are by far the most affordable in the world. As a result, as it happened with zero, the India Stack ecosystem is rapidly spreading around the world.

India's startup ecosystem has thus become a tremendous force for global good. The affordable digital products and services pouring forth from our entrepreneurial companies are solving the problems faced by value-seeking (*paisa vasool*) consumers worldwide. These solutions cannot be developed in Silicon Valley or other entrepreneurial clusters in the Global North.* Simply put, the problems of Jhanda Chowk in Hazaribagh cannot be solved in Union Square, NYC. By focusing on delivering affordable and scalable digitization, India has become the innovation hub for the Global South.

Similarly, India must become the innovation hub for affordable green technologies too. These technologies can be a vast resource for our country and drive growth. Solar trees situated on agricultural land could generate power for the grid and provide electricity for solar-based irrigation systems. Rooftop solar energy systems can generate household power and charge electric vehicles. The batteries in EVs can then be used during peak times to feed electricity back into the grid. Aggregating this battery power from millions of vehicles could produce substantial available power and displace expensive, polluting diesel gen-sets. Our startups now need

---

*Throughout this book, Global North refers to the thirty high-income countries (using the World Bank classification system) that are members of the Organization for Economic Cooperation and Development (OECD). All other countries, except for China, are defined as belonging to the Global South. China is referred to separately in all cases.

to take these technologies and package them with the right installation, servicing and financing services to deliver highly affordable solutions to the people.

Green hydrogen and bio-fuels are excellent dense energy sources for various types of vehicles ranging from heavy trucks to earth-moving equipment to airplanes. These new fuels are maturing quickly and soon will be cost-competitive with fossil fuels. However, we have not yet built the full value chain to make these energy sources convenient to use and affordable for the full range of possible customers. Entrepreneurs will have to drive down the cost of these energy sources through R&D and then establish manufacturing sites that can scale up green production. These fuels must then be made available at fuelling stations and depots. The National Green Hydrogen Mission (NGHM) will provide substantial incentives to develop affordable hydrolyzers, and many different concessional financing mechanisms are available for setting up manufacturing plants. Since renewables will soon account for most of our electricity generation, India can become a major exporter of green fuels.

Waste management and material recycling solutions are also emerging as major global industries. Unlike the Global North, which has large-scale waste management units, the Global South will likely have distributed waste management facilities at the village or neighbourhood level. However, these compact waste management plants have not yet been developed and tied into municipal garbage systems. Today, garbage in our towns and villages is simply picked up and deposited in the festering garbage sites that usually lie just outside residential areas. Entrepreneurs will have to invent systems to recycle valuable garbage (such as batteries, plastics and paper) while safely incinerating other types of garbage. Municipalities will need to come up with innovative billing approaches to pay for these services. Significant policy innovation is required in this area, but Indian solutions could serve as examples for the rest of the Global South.

Packaged foods are another major green industry opportunity. Many new technologies are transforming Indian agriculture, including hydroponic farming, efficient dairying, drones, new crop varieties and organic cultivation techniques. The dairy and fishery products, fruits and vegetables produced using these new approaches can be packaged efficiently for urban consumers around the world. For instance, snacking cucumbers grown in hydroponic farms in Maharashtra can be beautifully packaged and transported to supermarkets in Mumbai and Dubai. Packaged coconut water from Odisha could be exported to Singapore. Our startups can seize these opportunities and make India into a horticultural and dairy hub for the world.

Finally, the massive shift to EVs opens up entirely new fleet-based transportation business models. EVs are far cheaper than fossil-based vehicles on an operating cost basis. They should be operated for as many hours as possible, which will bring down the total cost of transportation. For instance, if used 10–12 hours per day, the running cost associated with operating an *e-rickshaw* is 25 per cent of the cost of operating a petrol rickshaw. A ubiquitous fleet of e-rickshaws utilizing battery-swapping networks will change commuting patterns in our towns and cities. Urban consumers may abandon their motorcycles for affordable, convenient metro and e-rickshaw-based commuting. Similarly, a fleet of e-bikes operated by full-time delivery staff may be much cheaper than a fleet of petrol bikes used by gig workers being paid on a per-trip basis.

Indian entrepreneurs can build large, profitable companies by targeting these massive global green markets. Their business models should be fully digital and designed around decarbonizing technologies. These green unicorns could drive decades of economic growth for India. They will create lakhs of green jobs, save tons of carbon emissions and generate lakhs of crores of wealth for the country.

Our book delves directly into the minds and experiences of the entrepreneurs leading the green crusade. In a series of engaging interviews, founders provide insights on how their innovations are reshaping industries – from battery swapping and sustainable agriculture to precision fermentation and sustainable lifestyles and beyond. Each conversation reveals these pioneers' unique challenges and triumphs as they work to transform India, one solution at a time.

These interviews open up windows into the passion, resilience and strategic thinking that drive these outstanding entrepreneurs. The individuals featured in this book embody the spirit of innovation necessary for addressing the complex climate challenges facing India. Through their first-hand experiences, emerge the technologies, business models and the deep passion that will shape our collective future. Together, their stories paint a hopeful picture of what a sylvan future for India could look like and what it takes to get there.

Selecting the Right Startups

As discussed earlier, the climate tech landscape in India is exploding, and selecting the right startups for this book was both a difficult as well as a rewarding exercise. There was both an art and a science associated with the selection process, with the primary goal of identifying startups that combined financial success with significant climate impact.

India's transition towards sustainable development has gained significant momentum in recent years. Government initiatives like the National Action Plan on Climate Change ('NAPCC') and its ambitious target to achieve 500 GW of renewable energy by 2030 have already laid a strong foundation. Moreover, the increasing public awareness and demand for sustainable products and services have also created a fertile ground for climate tech startups.

The good news is that startups nationwide are rising to the challenge. Through this book, we seek to investigate and profile startups that are pioneers in this historic transformation. Note that climate tech startups are not just an exciting investment opportunity, but also a critical pillar in India's fight against climate change. The entrepreneurs chosen for this book are true trailblazers in this space, building businesses that align with global sustainability goals while solving pressing local problems.

Selection Process for *India's Green Startups*

Our selection process for the startups featured in *India's Green Startups* is similar to the methodology that is utilized by most leading venture capital funds to find promising companies. But we extended this approach to include sustainability metrics, such as reduction in carbon emissions and creation of jobs for women. In this manner, we strove to ensure that the most promising climate tech ventures are selected. Our comprehensive selection process includes four stages: Screening, Active Screening, Detailed Evaluation and Investment Readiness.

This structured, multi-stage approach was developed to ensure that every startup chosen for this book would demonstrate extraordinary business success and thereby contribute to the fight against climate change.

1. Screening: Casting a Wide Net

In the early stages of our selection process, we cast a wide net across many climate tech industries, such as electric mobility, renewable energy, waste management and sustainable agriculture. We analysed hundreds of startups (somewhere between 350 and 400 companies), including early-stage and more established startups, to thoroughly understand India's green innovation landscape. During the screening stage, we incorporated various sources to identify potential startups. These sources included industry reports, startup accelerators, academic institutions and our extensive network of industry experts. We aimed to cast as wide a net as possible and identify a diverse pool of startups with high potential.

At this initial stage, we focused on five main criteria:

1.1 Total Addressable Market

We assessed whether a startup could target large, addressable markets. Startups needed to prove that their solutions or technologies could expand beyond niche markets. Scalability was critical, especially for businesses addressing climate change, which requires global-scale solutions. We prioritized companies that had potential beyond India and could address international challenges as well.

1.2 Climate Impact Potential

Startups with a clear and significant impact on reducing greenhouse gas emissions or improving sustainability were prioritized. We sought solutions that could be scaled up to make a substantial difference in sectors such as renewable energy and waste management, where widespread adoption is essential to achieving environmental goals.

1.3 Founding Team

The strength and experience of the founding team were crucial factors. We sought teams with the expertise to scale a business and a deep understanding of their industry. A strong founding team is essential for navigating the challenges of scaling a startup, particularly in the climate tech sector, which requires both technical knowledge and business acumen.

1.4 Technology and Innovation

Innovation is a key driver of long-term success. We sought startups with breakthrough technologies that could revolutionize their industries. Startups with proprietary technology or defensible intellectual property were more likely to be selected, as they had a clear competitive advantage that could sustain their growth.

1.5 Business Model and Economics

A clear revenue model, strong unit economics and a path to profitability were essential. We focused on startups that could generate sustainable revenue streams, especially in capital-intensive sectors like electric mobility and renewable energy. Startups with financial discipline and a well-thought-out plan for scaling their business were given priority.

This initial screening helped us significantly narrow down the field. Out of the 350–400 startups we reviewed, approximately 100–150 proceeded to the next stage. These startups showed promising early-stage indicators, justifying further investigation.

2. Active Screening: Deep Dive into Business Models

Once we had a more manageable list of promising startups, we entered the active screening phase. This stage involved a more detailed examination of each startup's business model, market traction and financial health. We interviewed the founding teams during this phase to better understand their vision, strategy and execution capabilities. These conversations helped us gauge whether the startups could realistically achieve their long-term goals.

2.1 Revenue Model and Growth Potential

Startups needed to show a 20–40 per cent compounded annual growth rate (CAGR) over five years, to demonstrate financial sustainability. We focused on businesses with proven ability to generate revenue while maintaining healthy margins. The ability to scale revenues while managing costs was critical for long-term viability. Startups that showed clear paths to sustained growth were prioritized.

2.2 Customer Acquisition and Market Momentum

We also considered market momentum, focusing on startups that had already gained significant customer bases and were exhibiting rapid growth. 'Battery Smart' (Chapter 13) and 'BluSmart Mobility' (Chapter 2) stood out during this phase. Both startups had already secured substantial customer bases and showed signs of rapid growth in India's electric mobility sector.

2.3 Competitive Landscape

The competitive landscape was a crucial consideration. Startups with clear competitive advantages – whether through technology, market positioning or partnerships – are more likely to succeed in the long term. We sought startups that had developed strong intellectual property or proprietary technology that gave them an edge over competitors. 'Log9 Materials' (Chapter 10) stood out as an example during this stage. This startup's remarkable progress in fast-charging battery technology using aluminum fuel represents an intriguing prospect to dramatically lower electric vehicle (EV) charging times. This advancement is transformative because it paves the way for a broader adoption of EVs.

During this stage, we also closely examined financial metrics such as revenue growth, working capital efficiency and capital expenditures. For instance, 'NeoCell Industries' (Chapter 7) demonstrated strong financial management with a capital-efficient business model and steady revenue streams from potential partnerships with leading EV manufacturers. Thanks to this strong financial foundation, NeoCell Industries is able to concentrate on expanding its advanced silicon NMC battery technology and establish itself as a frontrunner in the electric mobility sector.

Another standout was 'EMotorad' (Chapter 4). By focusing on manufacturing affordable electric bicycles, EMotorad is making green mobility accessible to urban and rural populations alike. What was most impressive to us about EMotorad were not just its innovative products and strong customer acquisition strategy, which have enabled it to expand rapidly into international markets. Its revenue model, blending direct-to-consumer sales with strategic partnerships, made it a perfect candidate for this book.

By the end of the active screening phase, we had further narrowed the field to ten to fifteen startups demonstrating financial viability and market traction.

3. Detailed Evaluation: Assessing Scalability, Efficiency and Governance

The detailed evaluation phase was the most rigorous part of our selection process. At this stage, we comprehensively analysed each startup's operational efficiency, scalability potential, governance structures and impact metrics. By the end of this phase, we clearly understood whether a startup could grow while maintaining both financial and environmental performance.

3.1 Scalability

Scalability was a significant consideration throughout this period. We evaluated the startup's solution's scalability within India and its potential for international markets. In climate tech, scalability is crucial for maximizing impact on climate. For example, 'Newtrace' (Chapter 11), which focuses on green hydrogen production, stood out due to its ability to scale its innovative technology across multiple industries, including heavy industries such as shipping and aviation. Newtrace's low-cost, scalable solution demonstrated the potential to reduce global carbon emissions significantly. Battery Smart (Chapter 13) also excelled in terms of scalability. Its battery-swapping network, which reduces the wait time for EV charging, is designed to be quickly rolled out across cities. This model is not only scalable within India but could also be expanded to international markets, particularly in developing countries where charging infrastructure is lacking.

3.2 Operational Efficiency

We meticulously assessed each startup's operational efficiency. Climate tech firms, especially those in the renewable energy and energy storage industries, are typically capital-intensive and require efficient resource use to maintain profitability. Over the long term, startups that demonstrated cost-effective operations were more likely to succeed. For example, *Log9 Materials* (Chapter 9), which specializes in rapid-charging battery technology, exhibited substantial operational efficiency, which allowed them to expand without overtaxing their resources.

3.3 Corporate Governance

The businesses selected were then evaluated on their governance practices. Startups prioritizing ethical business practices while maintaining transparent governance structures and establishing clear lines of accountability were more likely to attract long-term investment. Strong governance practices also ensured that the selected startups could manage the complexities of scaling while maintaining their mission of driving environmental impact.

3.4 Impact Metrics

We requested that founders submit quantifiable impact metrics to monitor their respective contributions to climate change mitigation. Startups were required to demonstrate that their solutions could provide tangible, measurable benefits through energy or water savings, greenhouse gas emissions reductions or waste management enhancements. For example, due to its innovations, *Nutrifresh* (Chapter 14) concentrates on controlled environment agriculture, providing explicit metrics for reducing emissions in the agricultural sector.

4. Investment Readiness: Preparing for Long-Term Growth

While *India's Green Startups* focuses on showcasing the most promising climate tech startups, we also considered each startup's investment readiness. Ensuring the selected startups were prepared for future investment was an important part of our evaluation.

4.1 Capital Requirements

Startups in capital-intensive sectors like energy storage or electric mobility often require significant upfront investment. We assessed each company's capital needs for scaling and whether they had a clear plan for deploying new investments. Understanding their cash flow and funding requirements was critical to ensuring they could continue to grow.

4.2 Legal and Financial Due Diligence

Each startup underwent rigorous due diligence to identify potential risks, including legal and financial reviews. This step ensured that the companies were prepared for the scrutiny they would face when raising capital in future funding rounds.

4.3 Valuation and Deal Structure

We assessed whether the startups had reasonable valuations and were prepared to negotiate with investors. This step was critical for ensuring that the startups were investment-ready and could navigate the complexities of future capital raises.

By the end of this phase, we had selected the startups that were having meaningful climate impact and were positioned for long-term growth and investment.

Conclusion: *India's Green Startups* Get Going

The selection process for this book was rigorous and designed to identify startups that could drive meaningful, long-term impact. By focusing on innovation, scalability and financial sustainability, we ensured that the startups featured in this book are well-positioned to lead the charge in India's transition to a sustainable future.

Each startup profiled in *India's Green Startups* represents a critical piece of the puzzle in driving climate action. They are at the forefront of innovation, developing solutions that reduce emissions and drive customer value. Through this book, we aim to showcase their journeys and inspire the next generation of entrepreneurs to take up the mantle in the fight against climate change.

1

Accacia's AI-Driven Revolution in Real Estate

Accacia is an AI-enabled platform that helps real estate and infrastructure companies (developers, asset managers, financial institutions, operators and governments) meet their net-zero goals.

Real estate and infrastructure contribute to 44% of global CO_2 emissions and, at current rates according to the company, it is expected to cost an astounding $24.2 trillion to get these sectors to net zero, making it one of the most critical sectors to tackle the climate change problem. Accacia's platform automates the measurement of carbon emissions for operating assets, and embodied carbon for under-construction assets. This allows accurate allocation of emissions for different stakeholders including asset owners, operators and tenants. Along with asset-level emissions, Accacia's platform helps asset managers track environment-related climate risks for their portfolios.

Accacia's story does not start with the typical entrepreneurial spark, but a moment of profound realization. An experience with flash floods in Indonesia opened Annu Talreja's eyes to the urgent need for change in the real estate industry. During her extensive career in corporate real estate, she saw first-hand the devastating effects of climate change. Real estate and infrastructure, were not just contributors to climate change through their emissions but also had an indirect impact on many other sectors. Annu knew that the consequences would be catastrophic if this sector didn't evolve. So she founded Accacia, a startup that uses artificial intelligence to help real estate and infrastructure companies track and reduce their carbon emissions.

We were drawn to Annu's journey because of her ability to combine deep industry experience with innovative technology while maintaining a razor-sharp focus on sustainability. By enabling companies to measure, monitor and, most importantly, reduce their carbon footprint, Accacia is revolutionizing the real estate industry. Accacia's recent $2.5 million seed round from industry participants is a testament to the potential and impact of its mission.

In this interview, we learned how, with the right vision and determination, even the most entrenched of sectors can be transformed.

1. How would you describe the climate change problem your startup is solving in India?

With its burgeoning population and rapid economic growth, India faces a unique challenge in tackling climate change. While engines of progress, our real estate and infrastructure sectors contribute significantly to national carbon emissions. This translates into intensifying heat waves, erratic rainfall patterns and increased vulnerability to natural disasters. The consequences are stark – impacting not just environmental well-being but also food security, water resources and public health.

At Accacia, we recognize the urgency of this crisis. We offer a comprehensive AI platform designed to empower real estate and infrastructure players in India and worldwide to track emissions from their buildings.

Accacia is a catalyst for a sustainable future, empowering a greener tomorrow. We enable businesses to transition from being part of the problem to becoming pioneers in implementing a solution. We believe in transparency, accountability and collaborative action, building a future where economic growth and environmental sustainability go hand-in-hand.

2. What was the spark that ignited your startup idea?

I had a bit of a non-traditional path to entrepreneurship. I studied architecture and urban planning and worked in corporate real estate for over fifteen years with companies like Marriott, AECOM and Ernst & Young. During the course of my professional life, I did many large-scale projects, like building hotels, industrial towns, etc. In 2021, flash floods in Indonesia massively impacted one such project. That was when I realized that climate change in the real estate industry was starting to have tangible impacts, and I wanted to do something about it.

3. Can you recall an 'Only in India' challenge you faced and the innovative way in which you tackled it?

One 'Only in India' challenge encountered was the issue of energy efficiency in older and traditionally built structures, which form a substantial portion of India's real estate. Many of these buildings, particularly in older city sectors and in rural areas, are not designed with modern energy efficiency standards in mind, posing a challenge to their achieving sustainability goals.

To tackle this, we developed a retrofitting analytics and guidance tool within our platform to address energy efficiency issues in these older buildings. The tool uses algorithms to assess the energy performance of buildings based on their design, the materials used and their geographical location, while also taking into account factors like natural lighting, insulation and existing heating, ventilation and air conditioning (HVAC) systems. This assessment generates customized retrofitting plans, recommending cost-effective modifications such as the installation of energy-efficient windows, improved insulation and integration of renewable energy sources.

Additionally, the tool connects users with local vendors specializing in retrofitting services, making it easier to implement these upgrades. It also provides a detailed cost-benefit analysis to help building owners understand the long-term savings they can make from energy efficiency improvements. Post-retrofitting, the tool continues to monitor the building's energy performance, offering ongoing feedback and additional recommendations, as needed.

This solution is helping bridge the gap between traditional construction and modern sustainability goals, which is essential for India's journey towards a greener future.

4. Imagine your startup as a character from Indian mythology. Who would it be and why?

If Accacia were a character in Indian mythology, I wouldn't just pick one – I'd envision it as a dynamic duo, an unlikely partnership that embodies the essence of our mission. On one hand, we would have the wise, resourceful Vishvakarma, the divine architect and craftsman. He would represent our data-driven approach, meticulously designing solutions to decarbonize buildings with pinpoint precision.

But what's a visionary architect without a bold, transformative force? Enter Hanuman, the god known for his boundless energy and unwavering dedication. He symbolizes Accacia's disruptive spirit and our willingness to challenge traditional norms and push boundaries in the fight against climate change. His agility and resourcefulness reflect our nimble platform, constantly adapting and evolving to meet new challenges.

Together, Vishvakarma and Hanuman represent the perfect synergy of wisdom and action. Vishvakarma provides the meticulous plans, while Hanuman infuses them with the power and momentum needed to break through barriers and achieve tangible results. This dynamic duo represents our mission at Accacia – which is to blend cutting-edge technology with a relentless drive for change, to be both the architect and the catalyst for a sustainable future.

5. Which global company do you admire or draw inspiration from, and what aspects of its journey do you wish to emulate?

The global company I draw inspiration from is Patagonia in the USA. Much like Accacia, Patagonia emphasizes social impact and community engagement. It's been a champion of environmental activism, and its 'Don't Buy This Jacket' campaign and commitment to ethical sourcing align with our belief in using business as a force for good, not just profit. Additionally, Patagonia's focus on transparency and trust-building through initiatives like its 'Footprint Chronicles' resonate with Accacia's data-driven approach. Patagonia's journey reminds us that sustainability and profitability can go hand-in-hand, and that's the path we aim to follow.

6. Paint us a picture of the opportunity landscape in India that your startup is tapping into. How big is it at this stage?

Envision a land of immense potential yet facing significant environmental challenges: this is India. In this context, our team at Accacia identifies a billion-dollar opportunity.

Our approach is grounded in a fundamental principle: effective management begins with precise measurement. Decarbonization hinges on accurate emissions tracking, a domain where Accacia excels. We offer the expertise and tools necessary to comprehensively assess the carbon footprint of businesses and industries, effectively equipping India with the tools for a sustainable transition.

With Prime Minister Narendra Modi's 'Panchtatva' initiative, which considers sustainability a pivotal pillar, India is poised for an eco-conscious transformation. This shift will be further bolstered by the growing demands for sustainable practices by international investors and trade partners.

The intersection of trade agreements, international financing and domestic pledges creates an unmistakable momentum for change. As a leading entity in India, Accacia is set to establish a high standard and spearhead the nation's journey towards sustainable development.

7. If your startup journey was a Bollywood movie, what would be its title and who would you cast as yourself?

If my startup journey were a Bollywood movie, it would be titled *She Builds*. I would cast Priyanka Chopra as myself, portraying my relentless drive to build Accacia from the ground up. The film would follow my journey as I enter the male-dominated real estate industry, determined to integrate sustainability into its core. Despite facing countless obstacles, I build Accacia 'brick-by-brick' into a global leader, redefining the future of sustainable real estate and proving that one determined person can truly change the world.

8. What myth about Indian climate startups would you bust with a fact or a story?

One myth is that all Indian climate startups are just copycats of Western models. The reality is that many Indian climate startups are homegrown heroes, tackling unique challenges with innovative solutions tailored to the local context.

Here's a story related to this. In a bustling Delhi neighbourhood, amidst honking rickshaws and fragrant samosa stalls, a young woman named Priya pores over data on her laptop. Priya isn't your typical entrepreneur; she founded Solar Saarthi, a startup tackling India's energy woes with a uniquely Indian twist. Tired of unreliable power cuts and rising electricity bills, Priya witnessed first-hand the struggles of small businesses and households. She created a revolutionary idea inspired by rooftop gardens: solar farms on wheels.

Now picture this: mobile carts equipped with solar panels, easily transported and deployed on rooftops across the city. These mini 'solar farms' would provide clean, reliable electricity, empowering local communities and reducing their dependence on the overburdened grid. Solar Saarthi isn't replicating a Western model; it's a homegrown innovation addressing a specific Indian need. Their mobile carts navigate narrow alleys where large installations are not possible, making solar power accessible even in densely populated areas.

Moreover, the company partners with local artisans to build the carts, creating jobs and boosting the local economy. Their pay-as-you-go model removes upfront costs, making solar power affordable for even the most marginalized communities.

Solar Saarthi is just one example of the many Indian startups in the climate change space forging their own paths. From using waste banana peels to create bioplastics to developing affordable cooling solutions for rural farmers, these startups prove that innovation thrives under the Indian sun.

9. Describe a day in your life as a founder in India – the chaos, the calm and the caffeine.

The first sliver of light peeks through my window as dawn breaks, and my day as Accacia's founder is already brewing. I have no snooze button – the city, the cause and a steaming cup of chai call out to me.

The morning buzzes with lively energy. My inbox brims with messages – questions from curious clients, updates from our tech team and other business partners. Each one needs attention, a piece of my limited yet ever-optimistic focus.

In the midst of this digital whir, I find peace in the quiet of data analysis. Charts and graphs become my roadmap, showing hidden carbon footprints, our solutions' potential impact and our progress. Every green tick, every downward-trending line, is a mini victory, a shot of espresso for the soul. But the real rush comes from the human connections – a call with a hesitant investor, their initial doubts melting into cautious hope as I share a vision of a cleaner, greener world with him.

The chaos picks up as the day goes on. Unexpected challenges pop up like monsoon storms – a tech glitch, a new regulation, a competitor's move. But amidst this whirlwind of activity, I find my centre. We strategize, we brainstorm, we laugh and sometimes we just vent. And then, with a final sip of chai, I close my laptop. The day may have ended, but the fight for a sustainable future never sleeps. Tomorrow, I'll wake up with the sunrise, ready to face the lively mornings, the quiet moments and the caffeine-fuelled quest to build a greener India, one eco-friendly brick at a time. It's not just a job; it's an adventure, a responsibility and a privilege. And I wouldn't trade that for anything.

10. If you could have a cup of chai with an Indian (or global) environmental icon, who would it be and what would you ask him or her?

If I could share a cup of chai with any environmental icon, the choice would be Sunita Narain, Director of the Centre for Science and Environment (CSE) in India. Her tireless work advocating for sustainable development and environmental justice makes her a true inspiration.

Over a steaming cup of chai, I'd be eager to ask her several questions, including what she sees as India's biggest environmental challenges and how technology can help overcome them. I'd also be curious to know what, in her view, are the most effective strategies for engaging young people in the fight for environmental protection.

I also believe the mere opportunity to converse with Sunita Narain and absorb her knowledge, passion and strategic insights would be an immense privilege. Her dedication to environmental justice aligns perfectly with Accacia's mission, and I'm confident such a conversation would be enriching and lead to further collaboration and a positive impact on India's journey towards a sustainable, equitable future.

11. Which book, movie or figure in India has left a lasting mark on your entrepreneurial spirit?

Amitabh Kant Ji, former CEO of NITI Aayog, India's premier think tank, ignited my entrepreneurial spirit. While he was not a traditional entrepreneur building a company, his relentless drive to transform India's economy and social landscape has deeply inspired me.

Kant's story isn't just one about founding a unicorn startup, but about leading revolutionary initiatives like Startup India and Make in India. He didn't just dream of a vibrant entrepreneurial ecosystem; he tirelessly championed it, removing bureaucratic hurdles, fostering innovation and igniting a nationwide 'can do' spirit.

He constantly emphasizes the need for 'out-of-the-box thinking' and encourages aspiring entrepreneurs to 'think big, think bold'. This resonates with my own journey, where I continuously strive to push our boundaries and find innovative solutions.

So, while Kant may not have built a billion-dollar company in the traditional sense, his impact on India's entrepreneurial landscape is undeniable. He's a true champion of innovation, progress and positive change.

12. Fast-forward ten years – What's your vision of your startup's impact on India's action against climate change?

At Accacia, we have been global since day one. Our startup's vision is to reduce worldwide carbon emissions by 5 per cent within the next ten years. This would amount to planting tens of billions of trees to reduce carbon emissions to this extent, which we believe we can achieve at Accacia.

13. Ever received feedback from an Indian customer that made you go 'Wow'? Tell us!

We don't really have a large customer in India yet!

14. Profit vs. planet – How does this debate shape your boardroom discussions?

The 'profit vs. planet' debate is often framed as a zero-sum game, but we see it differently in our boardroom. It's not a clash between two opposing forces but more like a symphony waiting to be orchestrated, where profit and planet can be harmonized into a powerful duet.

We reject the idea that we must choose between environmental responsibility and financial success. Both are essential and deeply connected. Focusing on one at the expense of the other creates imbalance in the long term. Instead, we strive for synergy by seeking out profitable and sustainable solutions. Embrace of sustainability can unlock new markets, improve resource efficiency and enhance brand reputation, all while boosting profitability.

We use data and analytics to measure our environmental impact and track the effectiveness of our sustainability initiatives. This data-driven approach informs our decisions and ensures that we are constantly improving. Our measure of success goes beyond profit margins. It includes carbon footprint reduction, resource conservation, social responsibility and the well-being of our team. A thriving business and a thriving planet go hand-in-hand.

The 'profit vs. planet' debate is outdated. In our boardroom, the music has changed. We're creating a future where profit and the planet work together in perfect harmony, enriching each other in a sustainable and successful balance.

15. When pitching to venture capitalists (VCs), what's the core story or angle you use to captivate their interest in your startup? How do you weave this narrative, especially in the context of India's unique climate challenges and opportunities.

As governments and regulators around the world impose stringent measures on the real estate sector to reduce carbon emissions, the focus is shifting towards robust, transparent systems for monitoring and reporting. These new policies demand that companies move beyond traditional, sporadic emissions assessments and implement ongoing, comprehensive carbon accounting measures. Just as every business relies on a financial accounting system to track assets, expenses and profits, today's environmental regulations necessitate a similar system for tracking carbon emissions accurately and reliably.

Accacia steps into this critical role as a dedicated carbon accounting platform, designed to meet the heightened expectations of regulators and stakeholders alike. Historically, corporations have leaned on Environmental, Social and Governance (ESG) consultants for periodic assessments of their carbon footprint. Yet, with ambitious carbon reduction goals now set, this periodic approach no longer meets the urgent demand for real-time, actionable insights. Continuous monitoring and targeted mitigation efforts are essential for progress, and platforms like Accacia's carbon accounting software as a service (SaaS) provide the tools needed to achieve this.

Accacia's platform allows businesses to adopt proactive carbon management, providing a centralized system for real-time data collection, analysis and reporting on emissions. This continuous monitoring empowers companies to adapt and refine their sustainability strategies promptly, aligning with both regulatory requirements and long-term environmental goals. As real estate companies increasingly embrace these solutions, platforms like Accacia's are poised to become indispensable for businesses dedicated to building a sustainable, low-carbon future.

Accacia intends to be the single source of truth for real estate managers and investors to effectively measure, monitor and report their carbon footprint. It intends to capture Scope 1, 2 and 3 carbon emission data – Scope 1 being direct emissions from owned sources; Scope 2 covering indirect emissions from purchased energy and Scope 3 encompassing all other indirect emissions across the value chain. Through proprietary data collection and third-party integrations, Accacia enables continuous monitoring and reporting of emissions data, along with actionable insights for reducing them.

16. For aspiring green entrepreneurs in India, what's your golden piece of advice?

It's important to remember that the term 'green entrepreneur' has two key components: 'green' and 'entrepreneur'. My advice to them is to focus not just on the 'green' aspect but also on the 'entrepreneur' part because the ultimate goal is to build a successful business. It's crucial to focus equally on market fit, pricing and distribution as on the product.

17. If you could wave a magic wand, what one change would you bring to the Indian climate tech ecosystem?

I believe software is only part of the solution in climate tech. A significant portion of the solution lies in hardware and innovative technologies like advanced batteries, carbon capture systems and green hydrogen, which are essential for achieving meaningful impact. These 'hard' innovations often involve complex engineering and manufacturing, which makes them capital-intensive. Until now, most of the capital has been made available to traditional tech-like businesses, which typically focus on software or digital solutions that scale quickly, such as data platforms or energy management software. While these are valuable, they are not enough to tackle climate challenges alone. If I could wave a magic wand, I would like to see specialist funds support these 'hard' innovations, such as direct air capture systems, which actively remove carbon dioxide from the atmosphere and store it safely, rather than simply managing emissions data. These hardware-intensive solutions require substantial, sustained investment and can potentially drive transformative change in climate tech.

18. In your vision, what are the two distinctly different but equally successful potential futures you see for your startup in the next five years?

I envision building this company in India as a global real estate sustainability leader. However, I recognize that different paths could lead to the same vision. The traditional dream of every entrepreneur is to grow their business organically and eventually list it on the National Association of Securities Dealers Automated Quotations (NASDAQ). I aspire to be one of the few women entrepreneurs from India to achieve that. Another path could involve being acquired by a large company that already has the client base we aim to reach. Which path ultimately leads us to our vision is something only time will reveal. At the same time, we stay focused on our mission of significantly impacting global real estate sustainability.

Conclusion

Annu and Accacia's story is a powerful reminder that real change is brought about by those who understand the system inside and out. Accacia is an AI company taking big steps towards making the real estate and infrastructure industries a part of the solution to adverse climate change instead of adding to the problem. Annu Talreja wants to make sustainability a central idea in construction, and not an afterthought. As Accacia continues to grow, it aims to set new standards for how cities should develop in a world that needs greener answers. Today, Accacia, under Annu's leadership, is redefining what it means to be sustainable in real estate. Annu has spearheaded a movement to decarbonize the most difficult and influential sectors in India as well as globally.

2

How BluSmart is Electrifying India's Ride-Hailing Industry

BluSmart Mobility is transforming urban transportation in India with the largest all-electric, zero-emissions ride-hailing service that addresses both air pollution and sustainability. As one of the country's first full-stack electric mobility platforms, BluSmart Mobility operates a fleet of EVs powered by renewable energy, eliminating the carbon emissions associated with traditional rideshare vehicles. Beyond simply offering a cleaner transportation option, BluSmart Mobility integrates real-time data monitoring to optimize fleet efficiency, ensure timely maintenance and provide a superior customer experience. By focusing on EVs, BluSmart Mobility not only reduces pollution but also leads the way in India's shift towards sustainable, scalable urban mobility solutions.

But it takes more than just a solid idea to compete with existing industry giants like Ola and Uber. It takes vision, grit and an unwavering commitment to a cause. Punit Goyal and

Anmol Jaggi's objective was to establish a unique ride-hailing service that would transform India's fundamental concept of urban mobility.

Punit's journey into the world of EVs was driven by his deep frustration with the pollution and inefficiency plaguing India's transportation sector. In this problem, Punit saw an opportunity. Drawing from his extensive experience in the clean-tech space, Punit envisioned a ride-hailing service that wouldn't just move people from point A to point B, but would do so with zero emissions and a reduced environmental footprint.

Despite competing in a field dominated by well-funded competitors, BluSmart Mobility has successfully carved out a space for itself. By building a vertically integrated business model that includes everything from the EVs themselves to the charging infrastructure, BluSmart Mobility is tackling the issue of sustainable mobility from all angles.

BluSmart Mobility's story offers a refreshing take on what it means to challenge the status quo. Its story demonstrates that with the right combination of innovation, persistence and a clear vision, it's possible to compete with and disrupt industry giants. Through this interview, we discover how Punit Goyal, along with his co-founder Anmol Jaggi, is setting a new standard for what ride-hailing can look like in a world that's increasingly focused on sustainability and environmental responsibility.

1. How would you describe the climate problem your startup is solving in India?

The climate problem is global and not restricted to India alone; however, its effects are being felt across the country, with unpredictable, extreme weather patterns affecting public health and agriculture, which continues to be a pillar of the Indian economy. In urban megacities, there is the added challenge of dealing with road congestion and pollution. In India, the mobility and energy sectors account for nearly 12 per cent of carbon emissions, and the transportation sector's heavy reliance on fossil fuels constitutes 50 per cent of the country's oil demand. EVs offer a sustainable solution, running on electricity and eliminating emissions. BluSmart is on a mission to 'Decarbonize Mobility at Scale' with its 100 per cent emissions-free ride-hailing service and EV charging infrastructure network. BluSmart is set to address urban climate challenges by providing people a reliable and safe commuting option that runs on clean energy and is non-polluting for the environment, creating a win-win situation for consumers, who get to experience an exceptional commuting service too, all within a fully integrated, vertically aligned business model.

2. What was the spark that ignited your startup idea? Share that lightbulb moment with us.

I've been a serial entrepreneur in the clean-tech industry for over a decade, with my initial ventures being in the solar energy space, primarily building solar panels and exporting them to different markets worldwide, including Europe and North America. The idea for BluSmart came about as a result of thorough research on various transportation systems worldwide, from Uber to Hyperloop, transportation in London and the Delhi Metro. I happened to experience a Tesla in the US and witnessed a solar panel-powered charging station at Google's Mountain View campus. This triggered the idea of an integrated energy-infrastructure-mobility ecosystem powered by electric vehicles and built keeping Indian urban cities in mind.

3. Can you recall an 'Only in India' challenge you faced and the innovative way in which you tackled it?

Most users' ride-hailing experiences are unique 'Only in India' challenges. Unlike in Western countries, ride-hailing in India is plagued by high cancellations, unclean cars, unprofessional driver behaviour and drivers arguing with passengers about their payment methods and drop-off destinations. The root cause, we found, is that vehicle ownership – particularly of four-wheelers – is extremely low in India. Ride-hailing companies expect drivers to finance and own their cars, but this model strains drivers, whose primary skill is driving rather than managing finances or operating as micro entrepreneurs. This burden of ownership often leads to financial stress, affecting service quality and reliability.

BluSmart Mobility's disruptive model addresses these unmet needs in India's ride-hailing industry. At BluSmart, we operate on a lease model, eliminating the driver-partners' need to use their own cars. Our driver-partners no longer bear the burden of asset ownership, fuel costs or overwork. They can focus solely on driving. The platform offers flexible jobs with inclusive and equitable economic opportunities, higher earning potential and guaranteed regular payments.

Moreover, BluSmart has created a complete ecosystem: the fleet, the charging infrastructure, driver training and customer experience improvement. Our driver-partners are the true brand custodians of BluSmart and the change makers on India's urban roads.

4. Imagine your startup as a character from Indian mythology. Who would it be, and why?

BluSmart is akin to Lord Krishna from the Mahabharata. Lord Krishna taught us persistence, perseverance, focus, righteousness, consistency, discipline and innovation. BluSmart is built on all these pillars.

5. Which global company do you admire or draw inspiration from, and what aspects of its journey do you wish to emulate?

I have drawn inspiration and lessons from many great companies worldwide, and I believe there are key strengths to be learned from each. Uber, Google, Tesla's technological prowess; Amazon's customer obsession and 'It's Always Day 1' ethos; and Apple's sheer courage and brand-building through constant innovation and design thinking provide ample encouragement to me and the entire team as we build BluSmart.

6. Paint us a picture of the opportunity landscape in India that your startup is tapping into. How big is this stage?

The stage is huge! The EV market in India is projected to grow from $3.21 billion in 2022 to $113.99 billion by 2029. As the market expands, so will the EV ride-hailing sector. Apart from BluSmart, other industry peers are entering or already in this space, showing that the market is rapidly growing.

Five years ago, when BluSmart Mobility launched in 2019, we faced significant resistance from investors, as they were uncertain whether a model like ours could exist and thrive. However, long-term investors placed their faith in BluSmart, recognizing our focus on solving long-term challenges. The overall EV ecosystem in India was still in its developmental stages, with factors like government policies, battery costs and charging infrastructure being areas of concern for investors.

With India's EV policy and the global trend towards decarbonization gaining momentum, we now see many global investors – such as global energy funds, impact funds and climate-focused funds – showing faith in and support for our idea, eager to join our vision of decarbonizing India's megacities. BluSmart is leading the country to sustainable, reliable all-electric mobility while building India's largest EV charging super-hubs, establishing a fully integrated, vertically oriented business model.

7. If your startup journey was a Bollywood movie, what would be its title and who would you cast as yourself?

The title would be *Avsar*, and I'd cast Amitabh Bachchan as myself. BluSmart seized the opportunity (avsar) to build India's only vertically integrated EV ride-hailing service and EV charging infrastructure company with a born-electric approach. At BluSmart, our thesis was clear: it is crucial to decarbonize the mobility sector, and the electrification of mobility is imminent. BluSmart embraced the challenge of building an energy-infrastructure-mobility and technology company with a full-stack business model designed for success and scale. BluSmart took on the might of Ola and Uber and reimagined ride-hailing in India from the ground up for a better and more sustainable future.

Amitabh Bachchan resonates well as the lead in this narrative in our minds. Time and again, Amitabh has seized opportunities to change the face of Hindi cinema with his renewed approach to it. He is also one of the most prominent personalities in India, strongly advocating for social and developmental causes and raising awareness about them.

8. What myth about Indian climate startups would you bust with a fact or a story?

There's a common belief that 'doing good for the environment' can't be paired with a viable business model that addresses practical, real urban challenges. BluSmart's journey has proven this wrong. We've established a clear product-market fit, with our riders finding immense value in our service, particularly in tackling the commuting challenges in India's urban megacities – all the while keeping emissions at bay and not polluting the cities where we operate.

Our strategic partnerships, such as the one with Tata Power to source clean solar energy, have made BluSmart a trailblazer in becoming 100 per cent emissions-free in its operations. I firmly believe that businesses can thrive and make profits while also being mindful of the planet and the people they impact. Our growth, reflected in a 125 per cent increase in revenue over the last year alone, is a testament to our strong business fundamentals and commitment to sustainability.

9. Describe a day in your life as a startup founder in India – the chaos, the calm and the caffeine.

There's nothing else I'd rather do than what I'm doing now. Building and scaling organizations and watching ideas and innovations come to life is incredibly fulfilling. Of course, this journey comes with its fair share of chaos, calm and caffeine. Some days are so hectic that I don't even realize I haven't eaten all day (though I wouldn't recommend this to anyone!). My days are packed with travel, meetings, brand building and fundraising – all aspects of the business I'm particularly passionate about.

I also make it a point to read many books, articles and reports to stay in tune with the market and business landscape. Organizations must constantly innovate and keep their ears to the ground, ready to make agile decisions and course corrections when needed. Staying updated with everything happening around the world is crucial for this, and it's something I prioritize every day.

10. If you could have a cup of chai with an Indian (or global) environmental icon, who would it be and what would you ask him or her?

If I could have a cup of chai with an environmental icon, it would be with Narendra Modi. As India's prime minister, Modi has shown remarkable leadership in addressing climate change and championing initiatives for a greener, more sustainable India. From launching the International Solar Alliance to setting ambitious renewable energy targets, he has put India on the global map as a key player in the fight against climate change. His vision and commitment to sustainable development make him an inspiring figure for those of us working in climate tech. I would tell him, 'India should impose a carbon tax, similar to the ultra-low emission zone charge in London, for ICE vehicles in our megacities. How soon and when can we make this a reality?'

11. Which book, movie or figure in India has left a lasting mark on your entrepreneurial spirit?

Mukesh Ambani is the Indian figure who has left a lasting mark on my entrepreneurial spirit. *Shoe Dog*, a book that has greatly inspired me, chronicles Nike's journey as it took on giants like Adidas and Converse. On a global scale, Steve Jobs and Apple's story of challenging industry titans like Nokia, BlackBerry and Motorola has also profoundly influenced my entrepreneurial journey.

12. Fast-forward ten years – what's your vision of your startup's impact on India's climate-change action?

BluSmart's mission is to 'Decarbonize Mobility at Scale', and we are already making significant strides towards this goal, including completing 500 million clean kilometres and powering our fleet with 100 per cent renewable energy. In the next ten years, I envision BluSmart transforming how India commutes within its cities and being a leader in shaping solutions to achieve the net-zero-emission goals set by the Indian government. I hope BluSmart will be at the forefront of tackling climate change and driving impactful change for the nation and its people.

13. Ever received feedback from an Indian customer that made you go 'Wow'?

The beauty of being in a consumer-facing business lies in the countless opportunities I get to meet and interact with our customers. Not a day goes by where I don't receive feedback, hear about consumer experiences or learn about the improvements they'd like to see in our service. These interactions are among my favourite parts of the job. As I travel extensively, I often meet customers at cafes, airports or during meetings. Social media, especially LinkedIn, is another platform where I constantly engage with and learn from our customers, understanding why they love the brand and addressing any challenges they face.

Some interactions stay with me forever, such as the heartfelt feedback from doctors and healthcare workers about their experiences during the COVID-19 pandemic of using our service, or the stories from women who feel extremely safe and comfortable commuting in our EVs, even late at night. Hearing from our women-driver partners, who share their pride in being recognized for their incredible work, is equally rewarding. These moments recharge me and fuel my commitment to deliver on our brand promise of providing exceptional and sustainable travel experiences to urban commuters.

14. Profit vs. planet – How does this debate shape your boardroom discussions?

At BluSmart, the debate between profit and the planet isn't a choice; it is our commitment to balance both. We believe that true success lies in integrating environmental sustainability into our business strategy, ensuring that our operations not only generate financial returns but also contribute positively to the planet. Our core value, 'People-Planet-Prosperity', guides every decision we make. We are fortunate to have the support of leading climate-positive funds, investors and partners like Tata Motors, MG and BYD, who believe in our mission. This backing allows us to pursue excellence without compromising on our commitment to the environment or our financial goals. For us, profit and the planet go hand-in-hand, ensuring our sustainable and impactful growth.

15. When pitching to VCs, what's the core story or angle you use to captivate their interest in your startup? Tell us how you weave this narrative, especially in the context of India's unique climate challenges and opportunities.

While pitching to VCs, I focus on the 'why' behind what we do and the founding tenets of BluSmart, which are being born-electric, having a full-stack approach and building a vertically integrated ecosystem. It is important to convey that we are an energy-infrastructure-mobility company and to take them through our pioneering model of integrating electric ride-hailing and charging infrastructure, and how both are powered seamlessly through technology.

16. For aspiring green entrepreneurs in India, what's your golden piece of advice?

My advice is simple: put your head down, work hard and fully commit to the idea you believe in. Do not shy away from challenges and failures – they are the lessons and experiences that will take you a long way.

17. If you could wave a magic wand, what one change would you bring to the Indian climate tech ecosystem?

I would remove the fear of failure from the Indian climate tech ecosystem. Indian clean-tech VCs are way too conservative, and this change would encourage bold and innovative investments in the country.

18. In your vision, what are two distinctly different but equally successful potential futures you see for your startup in the next five years?

I see two distinct but equally successful futures for BluSmart: First, BluSmart could become a successful, scalable and profitable global brand in the energy-infrastructure-mobility ecosystem. Second, BluSmart could be a trailblazer in India, establishing the largest network of electric ride-hailing fleets and open charging stations for urban Indians.

Conclusion

BluSmart isn't just changing how we commute but is redefining what it means to move sustainably in India's busiest cities. Under Punit Goyal's leadership, BluSmart has proven that you can build a successful, scalable business while staying true to a mission of environmental responsibility. By integrating electrical vehicles into their fleet, which are then powered by renewable energy, BluSmart has significantly reduced carbon emissions while increasing operational efficiency. As of October 2024, BluSmart has delivered over 610 million zero-emission kilometres, delivering 18.7 million zero emission trips and resulted in savings of over 55,000 tons of CO_2. As BluSmart continues to grow, it's setting a new benchmark for the ride-hailing industry, showing that the future of urban mobility can be clean, efficient and truly impactful.

3

RevFin's Mission to Electrify India's Future

What distinguishes RevFin from other startups in its sector is its dual emphasis on environmental sustainability and social impact. RevFin is pioneering a transformative approach to sustainable mobility in India through innovative financing solutions tailored for financially excluded individuals, particularly those lacking credit histories, in rural and small communities. These solutions empower them to become asset owners, enhancing their socioeconomic status and increasing their income. By employing advanced technology and data-driven methodologies, RevFin streamlines the financing process, thereby increasing participation in the green mobility revolution.

Simultaneously, RevFin, by emphasizing EVs, contributes to reducing pollution and promoting cleaner transportation throughout India. This dual focus on economic inclusion and environmental stewardship positions RevFin as a crucial player in the quest for a more sustainable future.

When we first met Sameer Aggarwal, founder of RevFin, his unwavering commitment to addressing one of India's most pressing challenges – reducing vehicular emissions – struck us immediately. Sameer did not commence his entrepreneurial endeavours in the conventional manner of a startup founder. His journey to entrepreneurship was spurred by a profound yearning to confront the environmental and social issues surrounding him, even though he came from a background in banking and finance. His extensive experience of working with subprime customers in London, while as a banker at HSBC, gave him unique insights into the financial struggles of those at the bottom of the pyramid. Upon returning to India, he saw an opportunity to leverage his skills in a way that could make a meaningful difference to people in that category while also contributing to the fight against climate change.

Sameer's entrepreneurial journey is, thus, a perfect example of how combining financial innovation with a strong commitment to sustainability can lead to transformative change. RevFin, under Sameer Aggarwal's leadership, is leading the charge to make sustainable mobility accessible to everyone in India while also offering hope and inspiration for the next generation of green entrepreneurs.

1. How would you describe the climate problem your startup is solving in India?

RevFin is focusing on reducing vehicular tailpipe emissions. The transport sector is responsible for approximately

30 per cent of India's pollution. We are financing and leasing vehicles that replace those responsible for the highest emissions. Typically, these are small intra-city commercial vehicles, including two- and three-wheelers used for last-mile delivery of goods, three-wheelers used for passenger commutes and four-wheelers used as taxis and for last- and mid-mile deliveries.

We have even started financing batteries and charging stations to enable quick establishment of the entire ecosystem.

As of October 2024, we have already contributed over 1.8 billion zero-emission kilometres, saving over 133,000 tons of CO_2 emissions. Because of the number of vehicles financed and made available by RevFin, over 10 million people in India travel in electric vehicles for their last-mile commute.

2. Tell us a bit about the company. What was the spark that ignited your startup idea? Share that lightbulb moment with us.

RevFin is a digital lender providing commercial electric-vehicle loans and leases. Our customers are mainly financially excluded individuals who sit near the bottom of the pyramid. Ninety-six per cent of our customers live in tier-2, tier-3 and tier-4 towns, and nearly 85 per cent are first-time borrowers. Our loans allow customers to increase their income to 2.5x of what they were previously earning. They get their first formal loan and become asset owners. Thus, our loans significantly impact the socioeconomic status of our customers.

Since our loans are for electric vehicles, there is also a substantial environmental benefit. I was a banker in London, and when I got to work with 'subprime' customers I realized that no credible data was available to assess such individuals when they needed loans. That led me to experiment with various underwriting techniques, and I discovered that the best way was to understand personal behaviours that directly correlate with intention to repay. As I started building on this, the entrepreneurial bug bit me. I decided to return to India, as the problem was much larger here and needed to be solved.

One day, as we were planning to launch our operations, I met an EV manufacturer in Delhi. It was winter, when pollution in the city was at its peak. I could only see thick smog as I looked out of our fourteenth-floor office window. I immediately decided that we should focus on electric vehicles. This was one way we could help reduce the problem of pollution in Delhi and in India.

3. Can you recall an 'Only in India' challenge you faced and the innovative way in which you tackled it?

One of the biggest challenges we face as a business is that our customer segment, essentially at the bottom of the pyramid, does not trust the banking system. Because of this, they mainly transact in cash, so several customers prefer to repay their instalments in cash. This creates certain risks for our business. We have used several innovative techniques to change cash usage behaviour among our customers. We incentivize users to register direct debits and pay through banking channels. These incentives result in lower instalments and interest rates for them. We have also given them several payment options, including sticking personalized QR codes on their vehicles to help them receive UPI payments and providing them access to multiple cash payment points.

4. Imagine your startup as a character from Indian mythology. Who would it be, and why?

Maryada Purushottam Bhagwan Shri Ram. Shri Ram, a young prince, was sent into a fourteen-year exile. During this period, he endured various trials and challenges while forming strong alliances, which ultimately helped him rescue Sita from the clutches of Ravan. These exploits established Ram as a supreme being, or 'Purushottam'.

RevFin's journey has closely mirrored this. When we began, it felt like being in exile. We started by working with customers near the bottom of the pyramid, helping them purchase e-rickshaws, a segment seen as doomed at the time. Investment was hard to come by, partnerships were rare and even hiring was difficult. Along the way, there were larger hurdles, like the COVID-19 pandemic, during which our daily wage-earning customers lost all capacity to repay their loans.

Despite all these trials, we formed deep alliances with players in the electric vehicle ecosystem. These alliances helped us scale and emerge victorious, much like Ram's alliances led to his triumph over evil.

Now we are among the largest electric vehicle financiers in the country, with abundant investments and partnerships. Our early hardships paved the way, following in Lord Ram's footsteps.

5. Which global company do you admire or draw inspiration from, and what aspects of its journey do you wish to emulate?

I draw inspiration from two companies – Tesla and HSBC – both very unique and different from each other.

Tesla is the world's most valuable automaker. They had the vision to go against the tide and bet big on electric vehicles, and they dared to challenge the large incumbents. Vision and courage, combined with product innovation and relentless hard work, have made Tesla a giant and created a new category of vehicles. Many others, including the major incumbents, have followed Tesla in manufacturing electric vehicles.

HSBC, where I worked for nearly a decade, also inspires me. I admire HSBC so much for its strong and deep organizational culture. I often say that if you shut my eyes and place me in an HSBC building anywhere in the world, I'd recognize it instantly. Its organizational culture transcends international boundaries and local influences. Another key lesson I learned at HSBC is the importance of sustainability. The bank is over 150 years old and has managed to sustain itself through various crises. The desire to build a business that lasts for generations is a value I carry with me, rooted in my experience at HSBC.

6. Paint us a picture of the opportunity landscape in India that your startup is tapping into. How big is this stage?

I firmly believe that nearly all intra-city small commercial vehicles, including two-, three- and four-wheelers, will convert to run on electricity in a few years. By my conservative calculations, this represents a financing opportunity of nearly USD 100 billion between now and 2028.

These vehicles serve essential end-use cases, such as passenger mobility and mid-mile, last-mile and hyper-local deliveries. To scale our business, we partner with original equipment manufacturers (companies that produce components to sell to other companies that integrate the parts into their products), dealers, fleet operators and e-commerce companies.

Currently, nearly 55 per cent of three-wheelers sold in India are already electric. Two- and four-wheelers will soon see a similar level of adoption. Small towns in India have leapfrogged directly to electric vehicles for their last-mile mobility needs.

India has very low vehicle penetration overall. Because of this, I don't see electric vehicles only as an opportunity to convert existing ICE vehicles, but as an opportunity for people who begin to use vehicles in India to go electric right from the start.

7. If your startup journey was a Bollywood movie, what would be its title and who would you cast as yourself?

The Bollywood movie based on RevFin would be titled *Lage Raho*. Perseverance is the one word that truly captures our journey. We kept progressing despite the challenges, trials, tribulations, rejections and mistakes. I would cast a young Shah Rukh Khan to portray me on screen. I am personally very ambitious, with a deep drive and desire to succeed. Shah Rukh Khan reflects that same ambition, probably because he too has a deep desire to succeed. I imagine him singing '*Bas itna sa khwab hai*' while portraying me on screen.

8. What myth about Indian climate startups would you bust with a fact or a story?

It is widely believed that Indian climate startups struggle to secure funding from investors. When we started in 2018, we found it difficult to convince equity and debt investors to back us. It took us over three years to raise institutional funds. When we spoke to investors, we realized they had no solid thesis on the electric vehicles segment in India, and their view on the market size was extremely conservative.

Over $5 billion has been invested in climate tech companies in India in the last two years. At RevFin, our ability to raise equity and debt funds has improved significantly, with us raising over $80 million in the past two years. Looking back, I realize that good business models with scalable opportunities will always attract investments. Our initial struggle to raise funds was less about being in the climate space and more about how well we could convince investors of the market opportunity.

9. Describe a day in your life as a founder in India – the chaos, the calm and the caffeine.

Being a founder in India is easily the most exciting career choice. Each day brings new surprises, challenges, opportunities and new people. I start my days early, usually around 6 a.m. First, I clear my emails and assign tasks to my team members. I reach the office by 9.30 a.m. and typically begin by reviewing all the numbers, which helps me focus my attention where it's most needed. I plan my day, but I never stick to the plan.

During the day, I meet my teams, helping them solve problems, seize opportunities and review performance. Being a solo founder, I get involved in activities across all functions. I spend time with every functional team daily, constantly tracking the real-time progress of our operational teams. I spend a lot of time in WhatsApp groups, motivating employees or cheering on their performance. As an analyst by training, I also analyze a lot of data daily to understand how our portfolio performs, drawing new insights and sharing them with my teams.

I also interact with customers, partners and investors daily. As the face of the organization, I engage in media/PR activities, interviews and social media posts and attend events. There's usually a queue of team members waiting to meet me every day, often for OTPs that are delivered to my number! Amidst the chaos, I drink several cups of black tea to keep going. Despite the daily hustle, I remain calm, which helps keep the team focused on our goals.

10. If you could have a cup of chai with an Indian (or global) environmental icon, who would it be and what would you ask of him or her?

I am deeply inspired by Anand Malligavad's work in restoring Bengaluru's lakes. I believe that water bodies are the key to solving the world's climate crisis. Restoring lakes helps raise the water table and improves soil quality, supporting greener landscapes and encouraging more rainfall and favourable wind patterns. These factors are crucial in reducing pollution and regulating temperatures.

Being from Delhi, one of the most polluted cities globally, I can say that pollution is making it increasingly difficult to live there, despite the city's superior infrastructure, culture, history, food, schools and parks. I would love to contribute to reducing pollution in the city. My chai conversation with Anand would centre on understanding the processes he used to restore lakes in Bengaluru, so I could apply similar strategies in Delhi – or better yet, convince him to bring his expertise to the capital. Delhi has several lakes, most of which are completely dry. Helping to restore these would be a meaningful way for me to contribute to making my city healthier.

11. Which book, movie or figure in India has left a lasting mark on your entrepreneurial spirit?

My all-time favourite book is *The Alchemist* by Paulo Coelho, and that book defines my entrepreneurial journey. Paulo Coelho famously writes in the book, 'When you want something, the whole universe conspires to help you achieve it.' When I started my entrepreneurial journey, there were many detractors. People were surprised and shocked that I wanted to leave my high-paying corporate job in London to start a venture in India. Everyone I met thought they could influence me to change my decision. But when people realized that I was firm in my decision and that I really wanted to become an entrepreneur, their attitude towards me changed completely. Everyone started thinking about how to help and support me in my journey. In my early days as an entrepreneur, I found a few 'angels' who helped me along my journey and helped solve the problems that came with it.

The Alchemist also teaches us that opportunity is right here, next to us. It may take us time to find it, but if you honestly try to find it, you will. When I started my entrepreneurial journey, I had a high-level idea of what I wanted to do, with no specific go-to-market strategy. But over time, with my sincere efforts, I found the right opportunity to focus on and to scale RevFin.

12. Fast-forward ten years – What's your vision of your startup's impact on India's climate action?

RevFin is an ecosystem enabler. Through our intervention, the penetration of electric three-wheelers in India has increased significantly. In fact, over 55 per cent of three-wheelers currently sold in India are electric, which is 5x from when we started in 2018. While we have financed vehicles for over five years, several other financiers have also entered this segment, learning from our experience. Therefore, we have also made an indirect contribution to scaling this segment.

We would like to see over 80 per cent of intra-city commercial vehicles converted to electric in the next ten years through our direct and indirect contributions. As an organization, we aim to finance 10 million vehicles over the next ten years, saving over 20 million tons of carbon emissions annually.

13. Ever received feedback from an Indian customer that made you go 'Wow'? Tell us!

Mahesh is one of our early customers. A young man with two kids, Mahesh lives in a small town in the Indian state of Haryana. He used to be a barber by profession until he took a loan from us to buy a low-speed electric three-wheeler, colloquially referred to as an e-rickshaw.

When I met Mahesh he told me how his life was completely transformed within a week of taking a loan from us.

As a barber, he earned only enough to take care of all his basic needs. He spent everything he earned during the day on the same day. After purchasing an e-rickshaw with our loan, he started earning ₹700 per day within the first week. This was about twice of what he used to earn previously. He said, 'I have two kids, and I have already enrolled them in a school this week.' He further said, 'I spend ₹300, keep ₹300 aside for repaying the loan and the rest I save.' I was taken aback by the change in his and his children's lives and also by the clarity of financial planning he had.

I think about my meeting with Mahesh very often. The feeling that my work has changed someone's life is very satisfying. Clearly, there are some things money can't buy ...

14. Profit vs. planet – How does this debate shape your boardroom discussions?

Profit and planet – both, not versus.

The world today faces significant climate challenges. While our board recognizes that, we also have to ensure profitability. These days, investors focus on funding profitable ventures. Therefore, if we have to solve large climate problems requiring many investments, we must focus on profitability.

Only a sustainable business can create a sustainable planet!

15. When pitching to VCs, what's the core story or angle you use to captivate their interest in your startup? Share with us how you weave this narrative, especially

in the context of India's unique climate challenges and opportunities.

We always start our VC conversations by explaining our purpose – why we exist. Our core purpose is to solve financial inclusion by providing loans to individuals who otherwise do not get access to funds through traditional financial institutions. This can be due to their having no credit history, their limited banking transactions, low levels of education, their living in underserved geographies or their lack of language exposure. While this is a fairly large set of individuals, there are many different reasons why they may need access to credit.

When we decided on our go-to-market strategy, we identified the electric vehicle financing segment as one with a high opportunity for scale yet one with enough mitigants to keep our risks low. Financing electric vehicles, especially low-speed three-wheelers, gave us the perfect opportunity. A typical borrower in this segment lives in a small town, is in their mid-30s, has no credit history, has a bank account with very low transactions and typically earns ₹8,000–10,000 per month, in cash. Such an individual has no access to formal credit.

When we started in 2018, there was no organized market for financing electric vehicles. This was due to unproven products and technology, virtually no secondary market and a highly fragmented distribution system. Thus, both the customer and the product were completely excluded, financially. However, we quickly realized that there were limited last-mile mobility options for passengers in small towns, which created a huge demand for services provided by these vehicles. As a result, individuals driving these vehicles could earn ₹25,000–₹30,000 a month and become asset owners, leading to a huge upliftment in their socio-economic status. We immediately recognized that this segment – focusing on customer impact, environmental sustainability and low-emission vehicles – would rapidly and significantly scale. On the other hand, since the underlying assets yield high customer income, we were confident that the risks would be manageable. The lack of organized financiers in this space also meant we could help shape financing in this segment and create market leadership.

Besides positively impacting customers, we have also significantly contributed to environmental sustainability. We have changed the last-mile mobility habits of over 10 million people, who have collectively travelled over 780 million zero-emission kilometres in vehicles we have financed. This has also contributed to saving more than 73,000 tons of carbon emissions.

As time has passed, we've diversified into multiple product forms and use cases. One of our key priorities now is electrification of the mid-mile, last-mile and hyper-local delivery fleets in the tier-1 cities. Through this initiative, we expect to save over two million tons of carbon emissions over the next five years.

16. For aspiring green entrepreneurs in India, what's your golden piece of advice?

My 'green' piece of advice to green entrepreneurs is not to worry about the total addressable market (TAM). Clearly, the TAM is very high, but because the space is so new the market size is not clearly apparent. The market needs to be created. You will find it very hard to convince people, especially investors, about the market's potential size. Stick to your belief in the size of the market and work towards creating it. Don't be bogged down by detractors. When market creation begins, investors and partners will follow.

17. If you could wave a magic wand, what one change would you bring to the Indian climate tech ecosystem?

The Indian climate ecosystem relies heavily on technologies and product components imported from other countries. Most of the innovation is in business models and the use of technology. What I would like to see is indigenous research and development of products. This will require significant and patient investments. Therefore, investors in this space must also change their risk appetite and investment horizons.

I believe India is in a very unique position today because of its large, young and aspirational population. As the world shifts towards environmentally friendly products, India is well positioned to become a world leader in this space. For example, India has over 1,000 electric vehicle manufacturers. These manufacturers rely heavily on components like motors, controllers and battery cells, which are imported.

Prominent battery technology, like lithium-ion, was itself developed outside India and creates a reliance on import of components from overseas. The country can gain immensely if alternative-chemistry cells can be produced using widely available elements in India. Through indigenous development and manufacture of products, India can become a leader in global supply of electric vehicles.

18. In your vision, what are two distinctly different but equally successful potential futures you see for your startup in the next five years?

We are on a mission to revolutionize sustainable mobility and envision two distinct potential futures. In the first, we don't exist – meaning, we've been taken over or acquired by another entity that carries forward our mission. In the second outcome, we continue to scale, launching an IPO in the next two or three years and becoming the largest EV financing platform in the country – and, consequently, also one of the largest non-banking finance companies (NBFCs) in the country.

Conclusion

Under Sameer Aggarwal's leadership, RevFin is a driving force behind India's transition to sustainable mobility, financing EVs and transforming the lives of millions of Indians by providing them with the tools necessary to enhance their livelihoods and contribute to a greener environment.

RevFin establishes a powerful precedent for other startups in India to emulate as it expands by ensuring that clean transportation is accessible to all and, in doing so illustrates how finance can serve as an incentive for environmental and social advancement.

4

EMotorad's E-Bike Revolution for a Greener Commute

Upon meeting the four founders of EMotorad and discovering the deeply intertwined journey of friendship that led them to where they are today, we were truly captivated by their extraordinary narrative. Founded in 2020, EMotorad has quickly emerged as a pioneering player in India's EV market, particularly in the e-bike segment. The company is building the world's biggest integrated electric cycle gigafactory. In phase one, spread across 240,000 square feet, EMotorad's gigafactory will manufacture all giga components, including the battery, motor, display and charger, which are critical to EV production. With an initial production capacity of over 500,000 e-cycles annually, the gigafactory aims to meet the rising demand for alternative modes of transportation.

But the EMotorad story transcends mere product creation – it embodies the genesis of a movement that could redefine India's transportation approach and environmental footprint. The founders boldly confront an unmistakable challenge evident to all who step outdoors – the escalating environmental crisis driven by carbon emissions from conventional vehicles. Adi Oza, the co-founder, and the EMotorad team perceive this not merely as an environmental issue but as a profound opportunity to offer a solution that could yield a discernible impact. Enter the e-bike!

What sets EMotorad apart is its unwavering commitment to crafting e-bikes that are not only eco-friendly but also accessible and attractive to a wide audience. By impeccably blending style and utility, EMotorad has elevated the bicycle to a symbol of sustainable commuting. Since its inception, EMotorad has launched several innovative models designed for urban commuting, all aimed at promoting a greener lifestyle.

The resolve of EMotorad to push boundaries in the face of challenges is truly remarkable. This startup is not content with simply being another player in India's EV landscape; it aspires to lead a global transition towards greener, healthier commuting alternatives. Its vision goes beyond selling bikes by aiming to cultivate a culture of conscientious commuting, where individuals opt for e-bikes as a mark of their commitment to the planet while not foregoing convenience.

The fact that EMotorad has already contributed to reducing over 25,000 tons of CO_2 emissions speaks volumes about the impact this startup has made. With a growing network of dealers and partnerships, EMotorad is positioned to expand its reach and influence in the market significantly.

The journey of EMotorad stands as an inspiring testament to the extraordinary potential of purpose-driven innovation. It serves as a powerful affirmation that when dedicated individuals unite with a shared purpose, they possess the capacity to drive transformative change. During this interview, we witnessed how Adi and Team EMotorad are not only crafting innovative bikes but also spearheading a movement to revolutionize our collective approach to commuting, ultimately effecting positive transformation in the world.

1. How would you describe the climate problem your startup is solving in India?

To truly understand the climate problem we're addressing, just take a look outside. Everyone is talking about how the weather has become more unpredictable – either it's raining more than the usual or it is not raining at all. Rising summer temperatures are another clear sign of how serious the situation has become. This is a crisis we have created for ourselves.

In 2023, global carbon emissions from fossil fuels reached an all-time high, making it the warmest year since global climate records began in 1850. The average temperature was 1.18° C above the twentieth-century average and 1.35° C above the pre-industrial average. A quick fact check will show that China, India and the USA are the top three contributors to climate change, accounting for 42 per cent of global emissions. This problem must be tackled on a large scale, starting from the grassroots.

Carbon dioxide is one of the biggest contributors to climate change, with transportation accounting for 14 per cent of CO_2 emissions, and cars and vans responsible for half of that. We've helped save over 42,483 tons of carbon emissions. Our broader aim is to ensure the world has a sustainable, reliable and healthier commute option – healthier for individuals and our planet – so we can achieve the ambitious goal of a zero-carbon footprint.

2. Tell us a bit about yourselves. What was the spark that ignited your startup idea? Share that lightbulb moment with us.

Talking about myself alone won't cut it because this journey wasn't just mine; it was a collective spark that ignited in all of us. One idea, one call and the next thing we knew, we were all hopping on the earliest flight, not to chat about the idea but to figure out when and how to turn it into a reality. The goal was to craft something to pull the world away from the clutches of carbon, plastics and other planet-harming culprits. It was our calling in many ways, and what we are trying to build is a call to action that our world desperately needs.

I am amazed at how easily change is triggered once you commit to it. It all began with a simple phone call, and now, together, we're steering not just my path or yours but everyone's journey towards a greener future. In the beginning, we were four people, and today the team is 200 strong, and has already convinced 1,00,000 people to choose e-bikes over cars and vans, which are major contributors to climate change. You can call me a climate change warrior, but I am one of many, just like Sandiip (Bhammer), my partners and our strong team.

3. Can you recall an 'Only in India' challenge you faced and the innovative way in which you tackled it?

It would be funny if I said there was just one challenge. Did you know India generates around 3.4 million tons of plastic waste, but we recycle less than 30 per cent of it? We couldn't sit back without contributing to the solution, but India needed to be ready for this change. Firstly, the infrastructure – there were no charging stations. Our solution? We created removable batteries that could be mounted and easily locked in place in seconds, which also worked as a solution for theft protection.

The second challenge was the high cost of electric bikes compared to petrol bikes in a price-sensitive market. We capitalized on the initiatives the Government of India had launched to make e-bikes more affordable for the masses. One such measure is exemption of capital goods and machinery required to produce lithium-ion cells used in EV batteries which has helped reduce production costs. For instance, a typical petrol bike may be priced between ₹70,000 to ₹1,00,000, whereas a comparable e-bike can now range from ₹30,000 to ₹60,000, depending on the model and specifications.

Other challenges included the lack of awareness among people and the limited bike range. We spent a lot of time creating iconic bikes that stood out in the market (for looks, and hey, you gotta show off, right?) while catering to different specs and price ranges.

4. Imagine your startup as a character from Indian mythology. Who would it be, and why?

If I had to choose, our startup would be like Shri Krishna. Although Krishna is revered as a God in Hindu mythology, I am more inspired by his principles and the role he played amid chaos. He played a pivotal role as a mentor, with a strategic vision and the ability to understand complex situations and provide clear direction. His guidance strengthened the Pandavas' alliance against the Kurus, even when the odds were not in their favour. He was the charioteer of change.

Similarly, when we started out, many sceptics questioned the viability of our venture. But, like Shri Krishna, we envisioned a future that transcended present realities. We believed in the possibility of a sustainable future – a vision that is now becoming a reality. Our goal has always been to make commuting cleaner and easier, minimize our carbon footprint and promote a healthier lifestyle. Ambitious? Yes! But despite the many obstacles we faced, our unwavering commitment to our purpose has driven us to persevere and achieve meaningful progress.

5. Which global company do you admire or draw inspiration from, and what aspects of its journey do you wish to emulate?

That's a good and common question that we are asked from time to time. But honestly, creating something better [than what existed] was the only idea we had for a better now, a better tomorrow and a better future. We weren't inspired by any other brand. Yes, some brands, I feel, are doing superbly in their fields. But at the end of the day, our prime goal was to craft electric cycles and ride them into a brand, and I firmly believe we have established that today. Yes, there is still a lot that needs to be done.

Speaking of emulation, we have always been determined to create everything that is uniquely ours, from product to journey. Because a copy is always a copy, and an original is, well, you know . . . So, yes, we are solely crafting our own journeys, and by 'our own', I mean EMotorad's own!

6. Paint us a picture of the opportunity landscape in India that your startup is tapping into. How big is this stage?

We come from India, but we aim to go beyond. It's for the world. We are working towards a solution that requires a collective, global effort for a cleaner tomorrow, given that rapid urbanization affects the world's major cities, creating traffic congestion and environmental concerns, not just in India, but everywhere. The Indian government's EV push through various initiatives, such as the Faster Adoption and Manufacturing of Electric Vehicles (FAME) scheme, which provides subsidies for electric vehicles, and the Production-Linked Incentive (PLI) scheme, which encourages local manufacturing of EV components, makes the process easier. With people becoming more environmentally conscious, we are on a journey that will change how we commute forever.

Electric cycles address the last-mile connectivity challenge in urban areas. As cities expand, there is a growing need for efficient and flexible transportation options to bridge the gap between public transportation points and final destinations. The overall opportunity landscape for an electric-cycle startup in India is significant. The potential market size is substantial, given the diverse factors contributing to the appeal of electric cycles for the country and their adoption. We are looking at a major shift in how people think and commute.

7. If your startup journey was a Bollywood movie, what would be its title and who would you cast as yourself?

If my life were a movie, its title would be *Babumoshai, Zindagi Badi Honi Chahiye*. This dialogue has long resonated with me and has shaped my journey. I have always believed in strengthening my roots while shooting for the moon. I don't subscribe to the concept of an 'ideal age' or 'ideal work-life' as a standard. I believe that standards can limit us, which is why everything I want to achieve, I aim for now. However, that doesn't mean I'm not humble about my beginnings. I believe nature is a great teacher and that we must nurture what nurtures us. I strive to make connections that are not ephemeral but genuinely meaningful, whether with colleagues, friends or subordinates. When you are truly there for people, you build respect, which is a wealth every leader should aspire to create. I am always expanding my circle and adding to the energy of creation. EMotorad is a testament to that growth towards sustainability.

My motto is simple: If the universe is ever expanding, why should we close up ours?

Which Bollywood actor should play me is an interesting question. Of late, whenever I see Vicky Kaushal on screen, there is an instant emotional connection, not just with the characters he portrays but with his personality as well. Since my story is also full of numerous twists and turns, each coloured with different emotions, only his versatility as an actor could keep up with it.

8. What myth about Indian climate startups would you bust with a fact or a story?

The most common myth is that climate startups in India face many challenges because of the low consumer interest in sustainable solutions. People are unaware that India had the first electric car long before the world saw it at scale. The success story of the Reva Electric Car Company, now Mahindra Electric, busts the myth that Indian consumers have limited interest in sustainable solutions. Despite the initial scepticism about EVs, Reva's introduction of the compact and affordable electric car, the Reva City Car, in 2001 demonstrated that there was, indeed, a market for eco-friendly transportation.

Consumers were receptive to the idea of electric mobility, and Reva's early foray into the market paved the way for subsequent developments in the electric vehicle sector in India. Mahindra & Mahindra, one of India's prominent automotive manufacturers, acquired a majority stake in Reva, reflecting recognition of the potential of sustainable transportation solutions.

It's true that the average Indian consumer is very cost driven and the market penetration of sustainable startups is slow. But the Reva success story showcases that when climate startups offer innovative, practical and affordable solutions, Indian consumers are willing to embrace sustainable alternatives. It highlights the shift in consumer preferences towards eco-friendly options and challenges the myth that there is limited interest in climate-change-friendly startups in India.

Today, Indian technology makes a significant difference in various sectors, including renewable energy, electric mobility and smart grid solutions, driving innovation in climate tech startups. Many of my fellow founders are sitting on top of some of the biggest tech advances the world has ever seen in climate tech startups. We are the same; our drive train technology will power everything that moves one day.

9. Describe a day in your life as a startup founder in India – the chaos, the calm and the caffeine.

You might expect me to say that as a founder, my days are flooded with emails and calls and spent in tackling unexpected fires. There are no lies there, but my days are filled with hanging out with my incredible team, discussing campaigns and solving their problems. Most importantly, I learn from them about how they work. The best part is when they keep asking us how we came up with the idea for the company or how we executed it. God, if only I had the bandwidth, I would answer all their questions. Oh, the tales I could tell!

As a founder, I can state that it is the most beautiful thing [to be a founder] because we have not only found a brand that is on its way to driving the world back to green, but we have also found a talented family that is now engineering these two wheels with us. Not to mention caffeine, which plays a huge role in helping me play my part!

10. If you could have a cup of chai with an Indian (or global) environmental icon, who would it be and what would you ask him or her?

I would say you, Sandiip [Bhammer], because you know how our conversations are always so mind-boggling.

Since I already do that often, I look forward to talking to Jadav Payeng, the 'forest man of India'. He planted a tree daily to restore his homeland and created a forest bigger than New York City's Central Park.

When he was just sixteen, he encountered a distressing scene on Mājuli, the world's largest river island in the Brahmaputra, where hundreds of snakes had died in a severe drought. Even at that young age, Payeng felt compelled to act. In 1979, he embarked on a mission to plant one tree sapling daily in the barren soil. Fast-forward over forty years, and his forest now spans 1,390 acres. Wow! This shows how big revolutions are sparked by a single step taken by someone driven to create change. His life will transcend him, and this is the kind of legacy we want to leave behind. I'd love to sit and chat with him about his vision and share ours with him – who knows what doors that may open for our beautiful planet. As Jean-Paul Richter once said: 'Do not wait for extraordinary circumstances to do good; try to use ordinary situations.'

11. Which book, movie or figure in India has left a lasting mark on your entrepreneurial spirit?

There are some books which, no matter how often you read, you learn something new from every time you pick them up. The Vedas and the Upanishads have always been those books for me. Ancient Indian texts are a profound source of inspiration for our lives, no matter what predicament one finds oneself in. While not conventional coffee table books or for light reading, these scriptures emphasize continuous learning, ethical values and a holistic approach to life. Entrepreneurs like me can draw insights from the Vedas' pursuit of knowledge and Upanishads' spiritual depth, encouraging resilience, innovation and a sense of purpose. The timeless wisdom of these texts leaves a lasting mark, guiding entrepreneurs towards ethical conduct, personal growth and a vision aligned with trying to ascertain broader meaning in their ventures.

I tell every entrepreneur that it's insane what our culture has to teach; undoubtedly, it has inspired the likes of Steve Jobs, Carl Sagan and Mark Zuckerberg. Every answer to your problems is right here, in the pages and pages of age-old wisdom.

12. Fast-forward ten years: What's your vision of your startup's impact on India's climate action?

[Taking] One step at a time, in ten years, we look forward to seeing all these small moves add up, creating significant change at scale and promoting sustainability.

Not to be boastful . . . but I believe we'll only be able to fast-forward and imagine a future ten years down the line because of sustainable ventures like ours. India's is a landscape with diversity at its heart; its topography and demographics vary at every turn. Still, a pressing issue unites us all: climate change has become increasingly harsh and impactful over the past few years. We chose electric bikes as our mode of transformation because they solve the congestion problems plaguing our metro cities and are carbon emission-free vehicles. With our various models, we aim to achieve widespread adoption of this vehicle, and hopefully, in ten years, we'll all be breathing cleaner air and driving freely amidst much more greenery than we see today.

13. Ever received feedback from an Indian customer that made you go 'Wow'? Tell us!

Of course, many stories leave us in awe. We connect with customers from all walks of life, starting from the grassroots, and one of our most recent encounters was with Mahesh, a Zomato food-delivery employee, who bought an electric cycle from us. He is visually impaired, non-verbal and lacks the use of his right hand, but despite his circumstances, he chose to contribute to the world meaningfully and inspire others by doing so. I think this is the highest form of feedback one could ever receive. Not only does it reassure us that we are on the right path, but it also shows that people believe in our vision. Stories like this one remind us of the profound impact our work can have on individuals.

14. Profit vs. planet – how does this debate shape your boardroom discussions?

A British archaeologist, Phil Harding, once said something amazing: 'Look after our planet, and it will look after us, or don't and face the consequences.' That's something so fundamentally beautiful and simple. If we live a life not worth living, how will any amount of profit matter?

Of course, philanthropy is not our only guiding ethos, but after all these years of running a startup, I have learned one thing: You cannot sell something you don't love, and when you love what you do, money follows, and invariably, so does profit. After all, my favourite quote to live by is, 'Do what you love, and you'll never work a day in your life.' The journey is so beautiful that I am not too worried about eagerly arriving at the destination.

Someday it will all pan out, but until then we're rolling down the road, wherever it takes us!

15. When pitching to VCs, what's the core story or angle you use to captivate their interest in your startup? Share with us your narrative, especially keeping in mind India's unique climate challenges and opportunities.

The core angle is the reality we face today. Nothing is more alarming than the dire consequences of climate change that we have created for ourselves. All the major cities in India have very poor air quality, with traffic congestion and rising population making an efficient solution the need of the hour. This is where we come in. We don't just want to reduce the carbon footprint; we also want to make commuting better. And by better, I mean more enjoyable. Given the unique terrain and demographic challenges at every turn of the road in this country, we're creating something you can ride to work on a Monday and then use to explore the roads less travelled on your weekends. The favourable initiatives of the Government of India have made it easier for us to penetrate the market and educate more people as we move forward.

16. For aspiring green entrepreneurs in India, what's your golden piece of advice?

For aspiring green entrepreneurs in India, my golden piece of advice is to take care of your people, and they will take care of your business. The customer is king, so treat them like one, but your team is the queen, and it's the queen who wins you the bigger games. Collaborate with like-minded individuals, leverage technology for eco-friendly innovations and build a business that thrives economically and contributes significantly to the planet's well-being. Stay committed, be resilient and always remember that each green initiative, no matter how small, positively impacts our world.

17. If you could wave a magic wand, what one change would you bring to the Indian climate tech ecosystem?

Even if I had a magic wand, I think it would take more than one change to make a difference to the Indian climate tech ecosystem. I would create a comprehensive and swift transition towards renewable energy adoption across industries if I could. This transformation would involve widespread implementation of clean energy solutions, fostering innovation in renewable technologies and creating a supportive regulatory environment. By accelerating the shift to sustainable energy practices, India could significantly reduce its carbon footprint and make substantial strides towards a greener and more resilient future. One can only wish for all these things right now, but someone has to dream a little dream first, right?

18. In your vision, what are two distinctly different but equally successful potential futures you see for your startup in the next five years?

I often tell my team that we are fortunate to be in a field with endless opportunities. This is the early stage of a major evolution in commuting, making it more sustainable, economical and accessible for a world population that's already over 8 billion.

In the next five years, I see two possible but equally successful futures for our startup. One path leads to significant advancements in battery technology and power transmission, making these solutions more evolved, efficient and scalable. Our R&D team is already working on several aspects including improving energy density, enhancing battery lifespan and optimizing charging times to create impactful solutions in the near future. The other potential future involves expansion into areas like recycling of battery packs, enhancement of after-sales service and development of charging infrastructure. The possibilities are vast – it is like asking in the early '90s what the Internet would open up. The answer is only limited by the extent of our imagination.

Conclusion

EMotorad truly embodies the spirit of Indian innovation in sustainable transportation. With a focus on accessibility and desirability, the company is leading the charge towards a cleaner future through electric mobility. Since its inception in 2019, EMotorad has rapidly expanded its operations across major urban centres in India, establishing a solid presence with a range of models designed for various demographics. The company's giga factory, which is under construction, will be the world's biggest integrated cycle gigafactory. With this expansion, India will be home to two of the world's largest gigafactories: one for Ola Electric two-wheelers and the other for EMotorad e-cycles. By combining style and practicality in their e-bikes, EMotorad is reshaping how people view environmental impact. The company's relentless innovation is not just redefining possibilities but also setting new industry standards in the fight against climate change, which is truly inspirational.

5

KisanKonnect's Journey to Greener Agriculture

KisanKonnect, founded in 2020 by Vivek Nirmal, is a transformative venture that is redefining the agricultural supply chain in India. Vivek Nirmal, formerly the MD and CEO of Prabhat Dairy, brings valuable expertise from his experience in the dairy industry to this new initiative. KisanKonnect directly sources fresh produce from farmers and provides phygital delivery to over 100,000 customers in Mumbai and Pune through its proprietary D2C app and farm stores. By collaborating closely with the farming community, KisanKonnect promotes sustainable agricultural practices while leveraging its in-house technology to ensure the delivery of fresh fruits and vegetables through an efficient channel.

Additionally, KisanKonnect offers curated agri-produce and handmade snacks under its 'Village Staples' and 'Mom's Kitchen' categories, supporting rural women who produce these items in a hygienic central kitchen. This dual focus not only enhances the accessibility of quality food products but also empowers women in rural areas, aligning with KisanKonnect's commitment to sustainability and community development. Through its innovative model, KisanKonnect is making significant strides towards bridging the gap between farmers and consumers while fostering a healthier and more sustainable food ecosystem.

When we first heard Vivek Nirmal's story about why KisanKonnect was founded, we knew he matched the profile of a green entrepreneur perfectly. Vivek's approach was to address the environmental issues of today and at the same time to reconnect people with their sources of sustenance. At a time when our food systems have become increasingly detached from food sources, Vivek's goal with KisanKonnect was to restore that link in a way that benefited both the environment and the customer.

Vivek's narrative is both motivating and practical for those who worry about how their behaviour shapes the planet. KisanKonnect is a completely integrated tech-based platform which ensures that consumers obtain fresh, responsibly grown food while helping to reduce carbon footprint at every point in the supply chain. It is not just another 'farm-to-table' initiative.

However, the path to establishing KisanKonnect was not easy. The agricultural sector in India is infamously filled with inefficiencies – from unpredictable weather patterns aggravated by climate change to the complicated logistics of shipping perishable goods over long distances. Firstly, addressing the serious issue of food wastage was critical, particularly in India, where over 40 per cent of fresh produce is lost even before it reaches customers. Secondly, there was also the question of transparency, as consumers have no idea where their produce comes from, who grows it or what the farming processes are.

KisanKonnect tackles both issues successfully. Their technology-enabled supply chain directly connects farmers with consumers, effectively reducing food wastage by minimizing intermediaries, responding to market demand, shortening transportation times, enhancing the visibility of produce and promoting local consumption, ultimately ensuring that less produce is wasted, benefiting both consumers and growers. On the issue of transparency, through KisanKonnect's 'Kisan-Trace' module, consumers are educated on the need for sustainable farming, which, in turn, creates trust among them. This approach to transparency, pioneered by Vivek and his team at KisanKonnect, has become transformative in a country such as India where customers increasingly worry about food safety and quality.

KisanKonnect is proof of the potential of innovation when rooted in tradition and driven by a clear purpose. More than a success story, KisanKonnect is a potent illustration of how businesses may effectively promote environmental change. With KisanKonnect, Vivek is not just building another startup but fostering a genuine movement towards a more interconnected and sustainable future for India in the matter of food.

Recently, KisanKonnect received $3.7 million from prominent venture capitalists and family offices to extend its climate-smart efforts in agriculture, highlighting the increasing importance of sustainability within the food industry. With this injection of funds, KisanKonnect will now be able to grow its operations even further and enhance its technology platform.

1. How would you describe the climate problem your startup is solving in India?

Imagine a human being eating fruits in the jungle some 20,000 years ago. There were no chemical fertilizers, pesticides, soil degradation, transportation, packaging and, importantly, there was no waste, as everything was consumed right where it was produced. Today, as civilization has advanced, we have created a carbon footprint just to stay alive! Our startup helps reduce this footprint across the entire supply chain of fresh fruits and vegetables, starting with nature-friendly growing practices. Our farmers regenerate the soil by using bio-fertilizers, and we've built a fantastic tech-enabled supply chain for fresh produce that connects farmers directly to consumers, significantly reducing food wastage.

2. Tell us a bit about yourselves. What was the spark that ignited your startup idea? Share with us that lightbulb moment.

In 2019, one of my father's close family friends passed away from cancer, and sadly, his wife also died some time after from the same disease. It really struck me then that our food has become so contaminated! It hits even harder when someone close to you is affected. This got us thinking about what we could do to make the farming of fresh vegetables more responsible and transparent. Coming from a farming family, I could see a big gap between the quality of produce at the farm level and what actually reaches the consumer. During one early morning visit to a local wholesale vegetable market, I saw a huge truckload of fresh fenugreek that had been dumped as a combination of sudden rains and low demand had led to its spoilage. That was when something clicked – we needed to create an efficient supply chain that protected produce from climate change and also benefited the consumer and the farmer.

3. Can you recall an 'Only in India' challenge you faced and the innovative way in which you tackled it?

There is an interesting one. It was actually a challenge our consumers faced. Our leafy vegetables are farm-plucked, pre-cooled, cleaned and packed immediately to retain their freshness. But some consumers started doubting their freshness, which was surprising to us. After digging deeper, we realized that in Mumbai, many leafy vegetables are grown alongside railway tracks in sewage water and sold in the local markets. While they look super fresh, they are highly contaminated and harmful. Some of our consumers were, understandably, afraid that they might be buying those greens. This insight led us to build a traceability module called 'Kisan-Trace', which directly provides consumers with information about the farm on which their produce is grown, the farmer and the farming practices they use, on our mobile app. We were the first in the Indian market to offer this level of transparency, helping our consumers truly 'konnect' with our farmers.

4. Imagine your startup as a character from Indian mythology. Who would it be, and why?

I think Kisan Konnect is more like Shabri, the devoted follower of Lord Ram. She searched through the jungle to gather fruits for him, tasting each herself before offering them to him to ensure he didn't have to endure even a bite of bitter fruit. Similarly, we take extra care in selecting the best-quality fruits and vegetables for our consumers. We sort and grade them, and ensure they reach our customers in the best possible condition so they only get the finest when they taste or cook them (of course, we don't take a bite before sending them out!).

5. Which global company do you admire or draw inspiration from, and what aspects of its journey do you wish to emulate?

I really admire Amazon for its boldness in imagining what didn't exist and for its use of technology to create that reality. We would love to achieve the same level of technological excellence in our own field and aspire to foster the innovative culture which is at the core of Amazon's success at KisanKonnect too.

6. Paint us a picture of the opportunity landscape in India that your startup is tapping into. How big is this stage?

We are a fully integrated company in the field of fresh agricultural produce, serving our consumers in an omni-channel way. So, literally, anyone walking on two legs with a mouth and a tummy is our potential customer in India. You can see the size of our TAM – the current estimated size of India's food and grocery market is $790 billion, with organized retail accounting for only around $68 billion today.

7. If your startup journey was a Bollywood movie, what would be its title and who would you cast as yourself?

The movie would be called *Mere Desh Ki Dharti*. The character playing me would be the son of a rural farmer who witnesses the impact of soil degradation on his family, community and village. He decides to ignite a revolution that eventually transforms into a movement, leading to substantial improvements in soil quality in our country. Through this movement, both farmers and consumers can begin to see a sustainable future.

Shah Rukh Khan is my all-time favorite. I'd cast SRK as myself, striving to do good for his country and his people.

8. What myth about Indian climate startups would you bust with a fact or a story?

Climate startup seems like a very catchy, hip and 'save the world' kind of title, even in India. However, you need to be very careful about your cost model. It's a myth that consumers in India are willing to pay that extra buck to buy responsible products. At least, not enough of them [are willing to do so] to make your business sustainable. So you have to mitigate those additional costs by bringing efficiencies into your business instead of loading them on to consumers.

9. Describe a day in your life as a founder in India – the chaos, the calm and the caffeine.

We have a super-energetic and fantastic team here at KisanKonnect. We believe in following the lead indicators – proactive measures that drive future success – of our business rather than the lag indicators, which reflect past perfomance. So, typically, our day involves reviewing consumer feedback, conducting root cause analyses (RCA) to pinpoint any issues and work on corrective and preventive actions (CAPA) to prevent them from recurring. We monitor metrics like fill rates (the percentage of orders completely fulfilled), delivery times (how quickly orders reach customers) and on-time deliveries (OTDs or the rate at which orders arrive as scheduled). Our goal is to keep improving, always striving to push our performance from 98.5 per cent to 99 per cent. The fun is in that last push! The calm, however, comes in the two days a week I get to spend with our farmers on their fields, tasting fresh veggies and fruits.

10. If you could have a cup of chai with an Indian (or global) environmental icon, who would it be and what would you ask him or her?

I would love to have a cup of chai with our prime minister, Narendra Modi. I admire his commitment to promoting natural farming and the support his government is providing in this area. If given the opportunity, I would ask him to channel the subsidies currently given to chemical fertilizers towards more sustainable farming models and to build programmes for their practical implementation. This would be a win-win for the soil of our country, for consumer health and farmer incomes; and it will even save the foreign exchange we spend on importing petrochemicals to make chemical fertilizers.

11. Which book, movie or figure in India has left a lasting mark on your entrepreneurial spirit?

I have been truly inspired by Dr Verghese Kurien's biography, *I Too Had a Dream*. It's amazing to see how one person can change a large sector like dairy farming and eventually influence the whole country. It shows that people can achieve anything if they act with good intent, conviction, sincerity and hard work.

12. Fast-forward ten years – What's your vision of your startup's impact on India's climate action?

More than a million acres of soil quality have improved in and around Maharashtra, and consumers and farmers benefit from the fair prices resulting from reduced wastage in the supply chain.

13. Ever received feedback from an Indian customer that made you go 'Wow'? Tell us!

I remember during COVID-19, one of our loyal consumers kept pushing our customer-care team to talk to the founders. When we connected, she expressed her frustration. She had been a loyal customer for a year and didn't know where to get 'Diwali faral' (traditional Maharashtrian snacks and sweets made during the Diwali festival). KisanKonnect enabled her to get fresh vegetables delivered, so she didn't have to go out, so why couldn't it address this need too? Interestingly, she was the one who gave us the idea to start our 'Mom's Kitchen' division, which engages rural women from farming families to make delicious and nutritious snacks, now supplied to thousands of our consumers every day.

14. Profit vs. planet – How does this debate shape your boardroom discussions?

To be honest, it's a balance we try to strike. I believe that if you have a sincere intent that benefits everyone, the universe provides you with the solutions you need. I can say that's what has been happening with us on many occasions since we started.

15. When pitching to VCs, what's the core story or angle you use to captivate their interest in your startup? Share

with us your narrative, especially in the context of India's unique climate challenges and opportunities.

Many investors are now aware of the challenges climate change is causing in agriculture, making our work easier. We generally tell them how KisanKonnect took shape as an idea, the kind of on-ground results it has produced and what it means for the future of the business. We emphasize the execution angle, because I've seen many good agricultural ideas fail because of poor execution. For us, execution is a very strong point.

16. For aspiring green entrepreneurs in India, what's your golden piece of advice?

My golden advice is to build a strong organization that excels in on-ground execution. A great idea is just the start, but success hinges on how well you implement it. Numerous challenges exist in the green sector, especially in India, including logistical, environmental and cultural problems. Without effective execution, even the best ideas can fail. So, invest in building a capable team and solid processes to bring your vision to life.

17. If you could wave a magic wand, what one change would you bring to the Indian climate tech ecosystem?

If I had a magic wand, I would build measurable monitoring systems for the entire farming process regarding its climate footprint. This would be an eye-opener for every stakeholder, highlighting the long-term effects of farming practices and climate change.

18. In your vision, what are two distinctly different but equally successful potential futures you see for your startup in the next five years?

I see our future in terms of our key stakeholders – consumers and farmers. In one scenario, I see KisanKonnect evolving as a responsible and most preferred partner for fresh agricultural produce in every household in Mumbai and Pune – the geographies in which we operate. Alternatively, I see KisanKonnect being recognized by farmers as a reliable partner in mitigating their agricultural challenges and successfully implementing climate-resilient farming practices to keep their soil alive.

Conclusion

KisanKonnect is an excellent illustration of how tradition-based innovation can create considerable environmental improvement. In an industry where trust is notably absent, by dedicating itself to transparency and traceability in the food supply chain, KisanKonnect is establishing new benchmarks that can transform India's agricultural landscape.

6

How CHUPPS is Redefining Sustainable Footwear in India

When discussing climate action, footwear might not be the first thing that comes to mind. But when you dig into the numbers – like the fact that over 2 billion pairs of shoes are sold in India annually, with most ending up in landfills within a few years – it's clear that even our shoes have a significant environmental footprint. That's why we were drawn to Yashesh Mukhi and his startup, CHUPPS. Yashesh isn't just making sandals and sliders; he's tackling one of the most overlooked environmental issues head on.

Choosing between fashion and eco-friendliness has always been frustrating for many fashion-conscious folks who are also concerned about the climate as they often have to choose one over the other. But that need not be the case anymore if startups like CHUPPS have anything to do with it. CHUPPS footwear is 100 per cent biodegradable (made entirely out of natural rubber) and breaks down in twelve to fifteen months without harming the earth. This is a game-changer in an industry where most products take decades to decompose (as a natural product, leather takes 10-50 years to decompose whereas typical polyvinyl chloride plastic takes 500+ years to break down in the same environment), releasing harmful methane in the process.

Yashesh's journey into sustainable fashion didn't start with a background in climate science or environmental activism. It began with the simple realization that India's open footwear market was ripe for innovation. The transition to casual, open footwear, which lifestyle changes and a younger demographic had highly influenced, had created a market gap. Yashesh recognized an opportunity to not only fill this gap, but also do it in a manner consistent with his values and the increasing demand for sustainable products.

CHUPPS's story is a sobering reminder of the significant influence our daily decisions – including something as mundane as the choice of flip-flops or slides we wear – can have on the environment. Our interview with Yashesh reveals how CHUPPS is leading the revolution in India's open footwear category by conclusively proving that style and sustainability do not have to come at the expense of one another.

1. How would you describe the climate problem your startup is solving in India?

In 2023, India saw the sale of 2.2 billion pairs of footwear. Shockingly, more than 95 per cent of these will end up in landfills, where each pair will take thirty to forty years to decompose, releasing methane, a potent greenhouse gas. CHUPPS is tackling this massive environmental issue head on. Our footwear is 100 per cent biodegradable and disintegrates within twelve to fifteen months and does not harm soil quality, eliminating a significant contributor to the product's carbon footprint. Moreover, our products are 100 per cent vegan, and all our packaging materials are plastic-free, further reducing our environmental impact.

2. Tell us a bit about yourselves. What was the spark that ignited your startup idea? Share with us that lightbulb moment.

India's open footwear (sandals and sliders) was traditionally limited to home or indoor use. However, lifestyle changes driven by a younger demographic, rising disposable incomes and the COVID-19 pandemic really accelerated the social use of open footwear. This trend created a demand for high-quality, affordable products, which created a gap in the Indian market. Most domestic brands focus on the lower-priced segment (lesser than ₹500), and the international brands are expensive because of high tariffs. That people regularly overspend on good-quality footwear inspired us to create CHUPPS, which could tap into India's large supply ecosystem and offer high-quality, affordable footwear to India's exponentially growing middle class.

3. Can you recall an 'Only in India' challenge you faced and the innovative way in which you tackled it?

A major challenge for us and other online sellers in India is high customer return rates, averaging about 30–35 per cent for footwear, mainly due to the cash-on-delivery (COD) purchase option. Customers returning products hurts profitability because of the additional logistics costs and the unsellable returned products, which is predominantly a result of incorrect sizing. To tackle this, we produced fun, educational videos on how to measure one's foot to order the right size, provided high-quality product images and videos, charged fees for COD orders and confirmed orders with customers before dispatching the product. Implementation of these measures more than halved our return rates to the mid-single digits.

4. Imagine your startup as a character from Indian mythology. Who would it be, and why?

We would be Lord Vishvakarma, the divine architect and master craftsman of the gods. Just as Lord Vishvakarma created magnificent cities and chariots, CHUPPS crafts meticulously designed footwear with innovative technologies, ensuring top-notch comfort, functionality and style. Known for its unmatched quality, use of the finest materials and creative designs, CHUPPS sets the gold standard in open footwear.

5. Which global company do you admire or draw inspiration from, and what aspects of its journey do you wish to emulate?

One company we draw inspiration from is Allbirds, a global leader in sustainable footwear, which has made remarkable strides towards carbon neutrality. They launched the world's first net carbon-zero shoes using innovative techniques and materials throughout the product life cycle. Their commitment to sustainability while delivering high-quality footwear aligns closely with our vision at CHUPPS.

6. Paint us a picture of the opportunity landscape in India that your startup is tapping into. How big is this stage?

India is the least penetrated large footwear market globally, with per capita annual consumption at just 1.2 pairs in 2022. Comparatively, in the same year, China's per capita consumption was 3 pairs, Brazil's was 4.5 and the US's 8. Favourable demographics, rising disposable incomes, lifestyle changes and government policies are expected to accelerate the market growth to a CAGR of 23 per cent through 2030, to a market size of US$ 90 billion. The casual footwear space, which CHUPPS serves, will represent a $68 billion opportunity by 2030, making India one of the fastest-growing footwear markets in the world.

7. If your startup journey was a Bollywood movie, what would be its title and who would you cast as yourself?

Swachh Grah, Sabki Bhalai. In our endeavour to reverse climate change, everyone must contribute to surmounting this challenge. We believe that meaningful, collective actions can lead to positive change, thus improving our lives and those of future generations. I would like to play one of the protagonists in the movie bringing about positive change. At CHUPPS, we are developing India's first fully biodegradable and affordable footwear, solving the issue of landfills. Making footwear affordable for most of the population will help bring about meaningful change. A cleaner planet will lead to better livelihoods.

8. What myth about Indian climate startups would you bust with a fact or a story?

The myth that many climate startups in India engage in sustainability greenwashing is misleading. While some may do so, most are making significant strides in reducing the environmental impact of business activity. For instance, using plastic-free packaging, CHUPPS saves over 30 kgs of single-use plastic each month. We also recycle over 800 kgs of waste materials every month to create new products. Recently, we introduced fully biodegradable footwear, which can significantly reduce landfill waste. These initiatives help lower our carbon footprint and demonstrate real, impactful climate action.

9. Describe a day in your life as a founder in India – the chaos, the calm and the caffeine.

Much like the famously unpredictable weather of London, a founder's day in India can feel like experiencing all four seasons in one day. Each moment demands agility and balance, from energizing the sales team and brainstorming with the product design crew to packing samples, updating investors and negotiating with suppliers. The daily hurdles and surprises can be daunting, but a strong sense of purpose and a positive mindset turn the challenges into rewarding experiences. Despite the lows, the highs and the sense of achievement one gets make the entrepreneurial journey deeply fulfilling and worthwhile.

10. If you could have a cup of chai with an Indian (or global) environmental icon, who would it be and what would you ask him or her?

It would be a pleasure to meet Greta Thunberg, the young Swedish environmental activist who has become a global flag bearer in her demand for climate action by governments worldwide. Her resilience, dedication and clarity have profoundly impacted my journey in raising awareness about these matters, educating myself and starting a sustainable business. I am particularly interested in delving into her inspirations and discovering the source of her courage to stand up for her beliefs against all odds. Her insights would be incredibly valuable to me.

11. Which book, movie or figure in India has left a lasting mark on your entrepreneurial spirit?

Aman Gupta, co-founder of boAt, has been a significant inspiration. Founded in 2013, boAt quickly became a global leader in consumer wearables, a space traditionally dominated by international players. Identifying a mid-market gap and delivering high-quality, affordable products with sharp marketing is what CHUPPS aims to emulate in the casual footwear space. Aman's incredible success in building boAt into a global brand in such a short time has left a lasting mark on my own entrepreneurial spirit.

12. Fast-forward ten years – What's your vision of your startup's impact on India's climate action?

Our vision is to emerge as a leader in sustainable fashion in India, with the goal of achieving a zero-carbon footprint. We aim for all our products and services to be carbon-neutral, positioning ourselves at the forefront of climate action within our industry. We aspire to create a platform to share our expertise and capabilities with our peers and policymakers, using our knowledge to help mitigate our overall carbon footprint. Real change requires collective action, and we are committed to driving that change.

13. Ever received feedback from an Indian customer that made you go 'Wow'? Tell us!

Last year, we received a DM from a woman in her final month of pregnancy saying, 'Your sliders keep us both secure and comfortable every day.' There was also a photo of her wearing our ERGOX sliders. She shared that she had regularly used our sliders for her morning and evening walks over the past few months. A few weeks later, she sent us another picture of herself at her prenatal class, all of them wearing our sliders. This put a huge smile on our faces and made our hearts swell with pride.

14. Profit vs. planet – How does this debate shape your boardroom discussions?

At CHUPPS, sustainability is at the heart of everything we do. Whether it's using plastic-free and recyclable packaging, avoiding materials sourced from animals, adopting electric transportation or developing fully biodegradable products, we always prioritize the minimizing of our carbon footprint. These measures do add to our costs and impact profitability, but we believe they are the right thing to do. As awareness and consciousness around sustainability grow, we expect more people to choose sustainable options, expanding our customer base. Ultimately, we see our commitment to the planet as a long-term investment in our brand's future and the well-being of our planet.

15. When pitching to VCs, what's the core story or angle you use to captivate their interest in your startup? Share with us your narrative, especially in the context of India's unique climate challenges and opportunities.

The footwear market in India is projected to be one of the fastest growing in the world, with a remarkable 23 per cent

CAGR expected over 2024–2030. This growth is primarily fuelled by low penetration, rising incomes and favourable government policies. CHUPPS is uniquely positioned to capitalize on this opportunity as the market rapidly shifts towards casual footwear. Our focus is on the underserved mid-market casual footwear segment, where we have established a strong presence through well-spread multi-channel penetration and robust execution capabilities. This strategic positioning is what allows us to fully benefit from the expanding market.

Additionally, we are working on several initiatives that set us apart from our peers. Our completely biodegradable products, use of innovative sustainable materials and adoption of eco-friendly practices in manufacturing and transportation give us a significant head start that will be hard to replicate in the short term. As adoption of sustainable products and brands grows, CHUPPS is poised to emerge as a leader in our category. By presenting a narrative of market potential and strategic positioning, and our unwavering commitment to sustainability, we captivate investors and demonstrate that CHUPPS is a smart investment and a driver of meaningful environmental change.

16. For aspiring green entrepreneurs in India, what's your golden piece of advice?

Purpose and persistence. Have a clear purpose for your business and a well-defined problem you are trying to solve. Stay persistent in executing your plans, even when faced with challenges. Sustainability is the way forward, and the support ecosystem for green businesses will only grow stronger in the coming years. Embrace your mission wholeheartedly and let your dedication drive you towards making a real impact.

17. If you could wave a magic wand, what one change would you bring to the Indian climate tech ecosystem?

If I could wave a magic wand, I would develop a robust funding ecosystem tailored for Indian climate tech startups. This would ensure easier access to capital for R&D and early-stage activities, which are crucial during the initial years when businesses aren't yet generating enough cash flow. Government initiatives, banks and private institutions could collaborate to establish dedicated climate funds, providing multiple avenues for entrepreneurs to secure essential capital. This influx of support would ignite a wave of groundbreaking solutions, propelling India to the forefront of global climate innovation and driving impactful change.

18. In your vision, what are two distinctly different but equally successful potential futures you see for your startup in the next five years?

In one future, CHUPPS will become the leading brand in India's casual footwear market, celebrated for our blend of style, comfort and affordability. We will dominate local sales and expand our presence across select international markets, bringing our unique designs to a global audience.

In another, equally successful future, CHUPPS will become a global leader in sustainable footwear. We push the boundaries of eco-friendly materials and practices, setting new industry standards. Our innovations inspire other brands, and we lead a movement towards more sustainable fashion worldwide.

In both scenarios, we are growing and driving meaningful change in the industry.

Conclusion

CHUPPS is proving that fashion and sustainability can go hand-in-hand. By creating stylish, biodegradable footwear, Yashesh Mukhi is reshaping the footwear industry and making it easier for consumers to make eco-friendly choices. CHUPPS creates a way for people to embrace sustainability without sacrificing flair.

7

NeoCell Industries' Bold Vision for India's Clean Energy Future

Neocell Industries is a cutting-edge lithium cell research, innovation and manufacturing company based in Andheri, Mumbai. Founded with the mission to establish India's first production facility for advanced Silicon-Lithium NMC (Nickel Manganese Cobalt) and LFP (Lithium Iron Phosphate) cells, Neocell Industries addresses India's growing need for high-density, durable and safe battery solutions. The company's R&D capabilities include producing up to fifty cells daily and offering flexible cell configurations to meet diverse industry needs. Collaborating with IIT and CMET for materials analysis, Neocell Industries is equipped with state-of-the-art facilities that support innovation in clean energy storage, with a goal to initiate commercial production by October 2025.

Neocell Industries' product line includes SNMC and LFP cells, specifically designed for applications in drones,

EVs, defence and other high-demand sectors. The Silicon NMC cells, among the cells with the highest energy density in the world, and the economical, long-life LFP cells prioritize performance and environmental sustainability. Neocell Industries' local manufacturing efforts aim to build a circular economy, significantly reducing waste and promoting recyclability within India's battery industry. With an experienced team from IIT, BARC and global collaborators, Neocell Industries is well-positioned to become a leading force in India's lithium battery sector, supporting the nation's push towards sustainable energy solutions.

Finding innovative, inspirational leadership is crucial in the ever-evolving landscape of clean energy. Chimanlal Gangaramani, founder of NeoCell Industries, embodies this blend of visionary thinking and practical execution. What caught our attention about Chiman bhai wasn't just his ambitious goals for NeoCell Industries but the depth of experience and passion he brings to the table. Chiman bhai's journey into the world of advanced lithium battery manufacturing was far from conventional. With a background in construction and project management across the Middle-East North Africa (MENA) region, he had already made a name for himself overseeing large-scale operations. But destiny had different plans, and his return to India marked a turning point in his professional journey.

Chiman bhai first learned about cell manufacture during an exploratory trip, to evaluate potential investment opportunities in emerging technologies, thanks to his now

CEO, Rushikesh Choudhari. This visit, which was more than just a meeting, was an introduction to the world of lithium cell technology and its vast potential in India. Although initially skeptical of the competitive landscape and the feasibility of entering such a specialized industry, Chiman bhai discovered something during this trip that ignited a passion for clean energy and advanced manufacturing. This encounter motivated him to dedicate over two years to researching the industry, both in India and abroad, to fully understand its complexities and the value it could bring to India's energy ecosystem.

Today, NeoCell Industries stands out for its technological advancements and the strategic foresight with which Chiman bhai and his team have navigated the challenges of the Indian market. From backing the right battery technology for EVs to addressing safety concerns and supply chain complexities, NeoCell Industries, under Chiman bhai's wise counsel, has systematically tackled each obstacle.

Chimanlal Gangaramani's story is a testament to how determination and willingness to explore uncharted territories can lead to groundbreaking innovations. For those who are passionate about sustainability and keen to see how big ideas can translate into real-world impact, Chiman-bhai's story is unmissable.

1. How would you describe the climate change problem your startup is solving in India?

NeoCell Industries, a leader in lithium cell research and manufacturing, is tackling one of India's most pressing environmental challenges: the overuse of fossil fuels in transportation and electricity generation. This widespread reliance on fossil fuels has led to severe air pollution and environmental degradation, contributing significantly to global warming. It's clear that reduction of carbon emissions is crucial to preserving our planet, and NeoCell Industries is at the forefront of this effort.

On average, each person in India generates about 1.32 tons of carbon emissions per year, with the majority of it – around 90 per cent – coming from fuel and electricity use. For example, just one litre of fuel produces 2.5 kg of carbon emissions, and electricity usage adds another 2 kg for every 200 watts consumed per hour. These numbers highlight the significant impact that everyday energy consumption has on our environment.

In India's transportation sector, greenhouse gas emissions from two-wheeler and three-wheeler vehicles alone exceed 35 million metric tonnes annually. However, NeoCell Industries' cutting-edge lithium cell technology offers a solution. By powering electric vehicles with these advanced cells, emissions could be slashed by an impressive 90 per cent, reducing these emissions to just 3.5 million tons.

This shift to electric vehicles – made possible by NeoCell Industries' innovations – would dramatically improve air quality in cities and towns across India. It represents a crucial step towards a cleaner, healthier and more sustainable environment for future generations.

2. Tell us a bit about yourself. What was the spark that ignited your startup idea? Share with us that lightbulb moment.

With over twenty years of experience in construction, manufacturing and project management as a vice chairman within the MENA region, I have overseen more than 11,000 employees and delivered high-quality projects on time. My journey began with a bachelor of engineering degree, leading to a successful career in the construction and industrial sectors.

Upon returning to India, I explored new opportunities that were beyond my established field. During this exploration period, I came across Rushikesh Choudhari, our current CEO, who introduced me to cell manufacturing. This 'lightbulb moment' was akin to love at first sight, compelling me to dive deep into rigorous research and feasibility studies for nearly two years in India and abroad. Despite the initial scepticism from peers and advisors, my conviction about pursuing this industry remained unshaken.

The journey has been challenging but immensely rewarding. Launching this project under the 'Make in India' initiative has been a proud achievement for me and my team, driven by the vision of contributing to India's self-reliance in advanced manufacturing and significantly impacting the global stage.

As mentioned, Rushikesh complements this vision with his expertise in material science. With over seven years in a C-suite position in the clean energy sector, he founded a solar company in 2013. Confronted with the inefficiencies of lead-acid batteries in solar projects, he sought better solutions. Discovering the potential of lithium cells and batteries, he realized they could address both current and future energy challenges, including those related to electric vehicles.

Together, we are committed to advancing sustainable energy solutions and driving innovation in the battery manufacturing industry.

3. Can you recall an 'Only in India' challenge you faced and the innovative way in which you tackled it?

We have faced our share of challenges but have emerged as a leader in India's EV battery industry through smart business strategies. One of the first hurdles lay in selecting the right technology for the Indian market.

After extensive research and a thorough understanding of the needs of EV manufacturers, we spent two years evaluating different technologies. The EV manufacturers ultimately chose Silicon NMC-based lithium cells, which are known for having the highest energy density in the world, effectively addressing the capacity limitations that plagued two-wheeler EVs. Safety concerns around lithium batteries – especially following reports of EV fires in India – posed another significant challenge. NeoCell Industries responded by launching the LFP and Silicon NMC cell series, which are among the safest in their respective categories. This move highlights our commitment to safety and reliability in the EV market.

Our startup also tackled the complexities of the raw material supply chain – a critical aspect of running a lithium cell factory. Drawing on the management's extensive experience in manufacturing, we streamlined the supply chain to ensure smooth operations. Additionally, we are working to establish a domestic supply chain for key materials that are currently difficult to import, so we can contribute to a circular economy and reinforce our commitment to sustainable practices.

Through these strategic efforts, we have successfully navigated significant challenges and solidified our position as a key player in the Indian EV battery market.

4. Imagine your startup as a character from Indian mythology. Who would it be, and why?

If NeoCell Industries were a character from Indian mythology, it would be Arjuna from the Mahabharata. Arjuna is known for his unwavering focus, exceptional skills and the relentless pursuit of his goals.

At NeoCell Industries, we embody these same qualities in our mission to revolutionize the battery manufacturing industry. Just as Arjuna was guided by a sense of purpose and commitment to righteousness, we are driven by our dedication to sustainable and innovative solutions for energy storage. Our precision, strategic thinking and determination to overcome challenges make Arjuna the ideal mythical representation of our startup.

5. Which global company do you admire or draw inspiration from, and what aspects of its journey do you wish to emulate?

While many global companies such as Tesla, Reliance, CATL, Apple and Virgin have compelling stories behind them and are highly motivational, NeoCell Industries draws the most inspiration from the Tata Group.

The Tata Group is admired for its unwavering commitment to quality, innovation and social responsibility. NeoCell Industries aspires to embody these qualities and become a trusted brand worldwide, prioritizing our country's and its people's interests. We aim to achieve a massive market size and offer groundbreaking innovations to our customers, much like the Tatas have across various industries.

Our vision includes improving human life and building sustainability into all our operations. By focusing on these core principles, we strive to make NeoCell Industries a world leader in the field of lithium cells.

Adopting a leadership style inspired by the Tatas, we are committed to ethical business practices, fostering innovation and contributing to society. These achievements will help us excel in our industry and make a meaningful impact on the global stage.

6. Paint us a picture of the opportunity landscape in India that your startup is tapping into. How big is this stage?

NeoCell Industries is strategically positioned to capitalize on India's growing opportunities in advanced battery technologies, particularly as a manufacturer of Silicone NMC cells for the two-wheeler market, lithium iron phosphate (LFP) cells for three-wheelers, and energy storage systems (ESS). India's strong economic growth and large population have created an urgent need for sustainable energy solutions, driving significant demand in several key sectors.

The EV market in India is booming, with the current battery market exceeding 20 GWh (gigawatt-hour, a unit of energy representing one billion watt-hours) and expected to surge to 150 GWh annually by 2030. Similarly, the ESS market is emerging rapidly, projected to surpass $5 billion annually by the decade's end. Additionally, sectors like railways and industrial and consumer electronics contribute significantly to the growing demand for batteries.

For NeoCell Industries, even targeting a modest 5 per cent market share in these expanding sectors represents a massive opportunity. Government initiatives such as the Faster Adoption and Manufacturing of Electric Vehicles (FAME) scheme, Production Linked Incentive (PLI) programs for lithium cell manufacturing and supportive EV policies bolster the sector's growth potential, providing a strong foundation for our success.

Moreover, our efforts are closely aligned with India's Sustainable Development Goals (SDGs), particularly in clean energy (SDG 7) and climate action (SDG 13). By meeting the rising demand for environmentally friendly energy solutions, our startup is not only poised for significant growth but is also contributing to the country's broader sustainability objectives.

As the demand for EVs and green energy solutions continues to rise, we are well positioned to thrive in India's evolving energy landscape. Our commitment to advanced battery technologies and our alignment with the national sustainability goals set the stage for our startup to impact the country's journey towards a greener future substantially.

7. If your startup journey was a Bollywood movie, what would be its title and who would you cast as yourself?

If NeoCell Industries' startup journey were a Bollywood movie, it would be titled *Shakti: The Power Within*. This title captures the essence of our innovation and our drive to create powerful energy solutions that can transform the nation. Aamir Khan would be an excellent choice for my role. Well-renowned for his thoughtful and impactful performances, Aamir Khan could portray the depth and commitment of the founder, showcasing the challenges and triumphs of steering a pioneering startup. His acting would bring to life the strategic thinking and innovative approach that define our company's journey.

8. What myth about Indian climate startups would you bust with a fact or a story?

One common misconception about Indian climate startups is that EVs lack the power and performance of petrol or diesel vehicles.

Ather Energy is breaking this myth with its flagship electric scooter, the Ather 450X. This scooter isn't just another

EV but is deemed to be a powerhouse on two wheels. The Ather 450X boasts peak power that surpasses many petrol scooters in its class, accelerating from 0 to 40 km/h in just 3.3 seconds rivalling high-end gasoline models. In real-world tests, the Ather 450X often outperforms traditional scooters, offering superior acceleration and handling thanks to its smooth and instant electric drivetrain. Beyond its performance, the Ather 450X is also more cost-efficient and environment-friendly, with lower operating costs due to the affordability of electricity and a significantly reduced environmental impact. This scooter proves that EVs can deliver a thrilling and reliable riding experience, whether in urban centres or rural areas across India.

Consequently, Ather Energy is proving that Indian climate-change startups can deliver powerful, reliable and sustainable solutions. In doing so, it is effectively dispelling the myth that EVs lack the power and performance of traditional petrol or diesel vehicles and is setting a new benchmark in the EV industry. This showcases that the future of transportation in India is both green and capable of high performance.

9. Describe a day in your life as a founder in India – the chaos, the calm and the caffeine.

A typical day in my life as a founder in India starts early with the calm and tranquillity of the morning. I wake up at dawn and begin my day with meditation, prayer and yoga, vital for maintaining balance and focus.

After this peaceful start, the day quickly shifts into high gear as I head to the office, navigating through the bustling streets. My workday is a blend of organized chaos – strategic meetings, problem-solving sessions and overseeing various projects.

Amid this whirlwind, I take time out for a quick chai break, which gives me a brief respite and a chance to recharge. I also prioritize quality time with my family in the evenings. Their support and understanding are crucial, offering me a comforting escape from the daily grind.

I watch television or indulge in stand-up comedy to unwind, which provides a perfect blend of relaxation and laughter. This downtime is important and helps me maintain a healthy work–life balance and keeps stress at bay.

10. If you could have a cup of chai with an Indian (or global) environmental icon, who would it be and what would you ask?

I would love to have a conversation with Elon Musk about climate change. I would focus on his groundbreaking efforts in EVs and renewable energy. Elon Musk has revolutionized the automotive industry through Tesla, advocating for the widespread adoption of EVs to significantly reduce carbon emissions from transportation. His vision extends to sustainable energy solutions, including solar power innovations through SolarCity and advancements in energy storage with Tesla's Powerwall and Powerpack.

Beyond automobiles, SpaceX, another of Musk's ventures, aims to make space travel more sustainable with reusable rocket technology. This innovation could potentially reduce the environmental impact of space exploration over time.

It would be fascinating to discuss Musk's thoughts on the policy changes that are needed to accelerate the global transition to renewable energy sources and explore how these strategies could be implemented in India. His insights on fostering innovation and overcoming obstacles in the renewable energy sector would be incredibly valuable for driving sustainable development globally.

11. Which book, movie or figure in India has left a lasting mark on your entrepreneurial spirit?

The Secret by Rhonda Byrne has left a lasting mark on my entrepreneurial spirit. The book's principles of positive thinking and the law of attraction have profoundly influenced my approach to business. It taught me the power of envisioning success and maintaining a positive mindset, which has been crucial in overcoming challenges and achieving significant milestones at NeoCell Industries.

It has taught me the importance of visualization, gratitude and unwavering belief in our mission. These principles have shaped my entrepreneurial approach and inspired my team to pursue excellence with confidence and determination. The lessons from this book continue to motivate us to strive for innovation and success.

An Indian figure I would like to mention – who has left a lasting mark on my entrepreneurial spirit – is Dr A.P.J. Abdul Kalam, the former president of India and a renowned aerospace scientist. His autobiography, *Wings of Fire*, has been a profound source of inspiration for me. Dr Kalam's journey from humble beginnings to becoming one of India's most respected scientists and leaders embodies the essence of perseverance, innovation and dedication. *Wings of Fire* chronicles his remarkable achievements and emphasizes the importance of dreaming big and working tirelessly towards those dreams. Dr Kalam's emphasis on self-reliance, visionary thinking and the relentless pursuit of excellence resonates with our mission at NeoCell Industries. His ability to overcome obstacles and his commitment to fostering scientific growth in India are guiding principles for our entrepreneurial journey. The lessons from his life and his contributions to science and technology continue to inspire us to innovate and strive for excellence, driving us to make a meaningful impact in the field of sustainable energy solutions.

12. Fast-forward ten years – What's your vision of your startup's impact on India's climate action?

In ten years, I envision NeoCell Industries as a cornerstone of India's climate action efforts, significantly contributing to the nation's transition towards sustainability. Our advanced lithium cell technologies will play a crucial role in the widespread adoption of electric vehicles, reducing reliance on fossil fuels and lowering greenhouse gas emissions.

We will also be at the forefront of the renewable energy sector by providing efficient energy storage solutions that facilitate the integration of solar and wind power into the national grid. This will enhance energy security and stabilize energy prices, making clean energy more accessible and affordable for all.

Our continuous investment in research and development will lead to breakthroughs in lithium cell efficiency, energy density and environmental friendliness, ensuring that our products remain cutting-edge. By establishing strong manufacturing capabilities within India, we will support the 'Make in India' initiative, creating jobs and boosting the economy while championing sustainable practices. Our vision is to lead lithium cell technology, driving innovation and excellence in battery production. We aim to set new industry safety, reliability and performance standards. Our commitment to sustainability will see us developing eco-friendly recycling processes, reducing the environmental impact of lithium batteries.

Through our work, we aspire to inspire other startups and industries to join us in building a greener, more sustainable future for the nation. NeoCell Industries' legacy will be one of technological innovation and environmental stewardship, positioning India as a global leader in climate action and sustainable energy solutions.

13. Ever received feedback from an Indian customer that made you go 'Wow'? Tell us!

Electronic vehicle manufacturers we have spoken with have expressed 'wow' and other surprised reactions upon reviewing the specifications of the lithium cells we will soon produce.

These industry professionals have been impressed by our innovative products and the advanced technology we bring to the market. Their enthusiastic responses have reinforced our confidence in the impact of NeoCell Industries' products. This feedback highlights the promising future we envision for our cutting-edge lithium cell technology in the electric vehicle industry and the energy storage and drones business.

14. Profit vs. planet – How does this debate shape your boardroom discussions?

In our boardroom discussions at NeoCell Industries, the debate between profit and the planet is a central theme. While financial success is essential, we believe that profit should not come at the expense of our community or the environment. We are deeply committed to integrating sustainable practices into all aspects of our operations.

For instance, our cleanrooms are designed to consume significantly less energy than current lithium cell industry standards demand, with optimized areas for maximum efficiency. Although it required extra effort and meticulous planning, our team has developed an advanced dehumidifier unit (DHU) that is exceptionally energy-efficient. This innovative DHU design minimizes energy consumption while maintaining optimal humidity levels that are necessary for lithium cell production.

This dual focus guides our strategic decisions and reflects our belief that success comes from positively contributing to both profit and the environment. By balancing our financial objectives with environmental stewardship, we aim to create long-term value that extends beyond the bottom line, fostering a sustainable and profitable future.

15. When pitching to VCs, what's the core story or angle you use to captivate their interest in your startup? Share how you weave this narrative, especially considering India's unique climate challenges and opportunities.

When pitching to venture capitalists, we emphasize both the safety and the highest return on investment (ROI) that's possible with our advanced lithium cell technology. We articulate how NeoCell Industries addresses India's unique climate challenges by innovating in sustainable battery technology. We highlight the vast opportunities in India's growing demand for clean and safe energy solutions for electric vehicles, showcasing our role in this transformative sector.

Our narrative focuses on our commitment to safety, reliability and sustainability. As India's first Silicon NMC lithium cell manufacturer, we lead the industry with the highest energy density cells designed specifically for Indian EV manufacturers. Our cells offer a longer life cycle than those of tier-1 manufacturers, ensuring better performance and greater value over time.

We share our journey of success, demonstrating our robust growth and the significant impact of our solutions in reducing carbon emissions and enhancing energy security. By combining a strong business case with our mission to tackle climate change, we capture the VCs' interest and confidence in our vision for a sustainable future. Our emphasis on innovative technologies and on addressing a clear market need positions us as a key player in the clean energy revolution, offering both financial returns and a positive environmental impact.

16. For aspiring green entrepreneurs in India, what's your golden piece of advice?

Whenever you take up a task, trust yourself and give it your 100 per cent. Stay focused, avoid distractions and remain dedicated to your vision. Success is bound to follow when you are committed and put your best efforts into your work. This unwavering dedication and belief in your mission are crucial for overcoming challenges and achieving your entrepreneurial goals.

Innovation is key to staying ahead in any industry. Always work on developing new technologies that can give you a competitive edge. Conduct thorough market research to understand the needs and trends of your target audience. Invest time in product research to ensure your offerings are of the highest quality and meet market demands.

Dedication, innovation and strategic planning will allow you to navigate challenges and drive your business towards sustained success. Remember, a focused and committed approach, coupled with continuous learning and innovation, is the key to achieving your entrepreneurial goals.

17. If you could wave a magic wand, what is one change that you would bring to the Indian climate tech ecosystem?

I would foster stronger collaboration between industry, academia and the government in the Indian climate tech ecosystem. The synergy between these sectors is crucial as it will bridge the gap between theoretical research and practical applications. Industry provides practical insights, resources and market-driven perspectives, while academia offers cutting-edge research and a deep understanding of emerging technologies. Together, they can accelerate the development and commercialization of sustainable technologies, such as advanced renewable energy solutions and innovative carbon-capture methods.

The government's role in this partnership is pivotal. By collaborating with industry and academia, the government can streamline regulatory processes, making the introduction of new technologies into the market easier. Additionally, government funding and incentives can stimulate further research and development, helping to de-risk early-stage innovations and attract private investment. Effective policies and regulations can ensure that deploying new technologies aligns with national sustainability goals and environmental standards.

This integrated approach will create a supportive environment for climate tech innovation, driving India's transition to a green economy and ensuring the country remains at the forefront of the global fight against climate change.

18. In your vision, what are two distinctly different but equally successful potential futures you see for your startup in the next five years?

When we look ahead at our company's future, two distinct yet equally promising paths emerge, each with the potential to significantly shape the clean energy landscape over the next five years.

In one scenario, NeoCell Industries becomes a market leader in EV battery cell technology in India. By capitalizing on our advanced silicon NMC cells, we deliver high-performance, cost-effective solutions that extend the range and lifespan of electric vehicles. This technology has become the go-to choice for major EV manufacturers, leading to strategic partnerships with top automotive brands and powering a significant share of new EVs sold in India. This success would translate into robust revenue growth and a commanding market presence, all while continuous innovation keeps us at the forefront of battery technology.

In another scenario, we could pursue pioneering of the 'perovskite solar cell' (a new, highly efficient type of solar cell that's cheaper to produce and can be made flexible, offering a promising alternative to traditional solar panels) technology in India. Recognizing the revolutionary potential of perovskites, with their high efficiency and low production costs, we could focus on developing and commercializing advanced perovskite solar cells. Our research could lead to groundbreaking innovations that surpass traditional silicon-based cells, enabling us to partner with solar panel manufacturers and energy companies. Integrating our technology into residential, commercial and utility-scale solar projects could help accelerate the transition to renewable energy, opening new revenue streams and ensuring sustainable growth.

Perhaps the most exciting possibility lies in combining these two futures, creating a powerful synergy between battery and solar technologies. By advancing both fields, we could develop integrated systems where high-performance batteries store energy generated by our efficient perovskite solar cells. This dual approach offers better ranges for electric vehicles and contributes to a more sustainable energy ecosystem. Regardless of our specific path, our core mission of driving innovation in clean energy remains at the heart of our strategy, ensuring that our future is diversified and aligned with global sustainability goals.

Conclusion

NeoCell Industries is transforming ambitious ideas into real-world solutions for India's energy needs. Under Chimanlal Gangaramani's leadership, this Mumbai-based startup is making commendable strides in both battery and solar technology by bringing clean energy closer to everyday use.

Every move NeoCell Industries makes is a step towards making advanced battery technology a key part of India's sustainable future and paves the way for a cleaner, more energy-efficient tomorrow.

8

Zero Cow Factory's Animal-Free Revolution

Our introduction to Sohil Kapadia and his wife Parini, who is also his co-founder, and their work at Zero Cow Factory was eye opening. This husband-wife team had a strong vision and dared to question one of India's most conventional, politically sensitive and deeply ingrained businesses – the dairy sector. If love for sustainability and creativity drives you, Sohil and Parini's path presents a fresh and motivating story of how novel ideas could totally change accepted wisdom.

Being a serial entrepreneur, Sohil had the understanding required to see how greatly the dairy sector affects our surroundings. He recognized a chance to address one of the most urgent problems in the world in an innovative manner when he learned about the possibilities of 'precision fermentation', a modern technology that allows the production of dairy proteins without involving any animals. It was a revolutionary idea – to create dairy products while completely cutting out the environmental damage caused by conventional farming. This thought inspired Zero Cow Factory – the first startup in Asia to aim at precisely fermenting dairy products without the involvement of animals.

Zero Cow Factory's approach is compelling because it strategically uses India's strengths. With the country being the largest producer and consumer of dairy and a rising bio-manufacturing hub, the founders recognized the unique opportunity to leverage India's scientific expertise, low-cost manufacturing and vast market to create a sustainable alternative to conventional dairy. Their mission was fundamentally about rethinking how we produce food to benefit both people and the planet.

Sohil and Parini's story is a powerful example of how a visionary idea, backed by the right technology and a strong commitment to sustainability, can disrupt even the most established industries. Their work at Zero Cow Factory is not just about introducing a new product, but also about redefining an entire sector and setting a precedent for future climate-conscious entrepreneurs. Sohil and Parini Kapadia are leading the charge in transforming our food systems in India (and, possibly, the world) for a more sustainable and humane future.

1. How would you describe the climate problem your startup is solving in India?

Everyone loves dairy products; they have the essential nutrients human beings require. But the downsides of animal agriculture are undeniable. Traditional dairy farming is hugely unsustainable. It's a leading contributor to greenhouse gas emissions and, in a very big way, consists of inefficient use of resources. India is known to be the largest producer and consumer of dairy with the highest livestock population (300-plus million). While dairy products are delicious, very few know that each cow produces upto 500 litres of methane daily, which harms our planet.

At Zero Cow Factory, our mission is to produce animal-free dairy proteins and products through precision fermentation technology, which is sustainable and better than conventional dairy farming for the planet and its people and animals. Precision fermentation is similar to brewing beer, but we produce dairy proteins such as casein and whey using advanced fermentation technologies that do not involve the rearing of animals. With the growing global population and resources becoming limited, it seems impossible to feed 10 billion people by 2050 through traditional means. The good news is that today's conscious consumers are more inclined towards using sustainable products and embracing veganism for various reasons. Zero Cow Factory firmly believes that the young population will drive the future demand for sustainable products.

2. Tell us a bit about yourselves. What was the spark that ignited your startup idea? Share with us that lightbulb moment.

I am a serial entrepreneur and have always been close to nature. As I sought my next venture, I wanted to address a significant challenge that could transform the next century by providing innovative solutions to the issues of sustainable food production and reducing the environmental impact of livestock farming. The first spark came when I learned that food could be produced from animals or plants using sustainable technologies like cellular agriculture, particularly in countries like the United States, Singapore and Israel. This is also known as the production of alternative proteins. That was my lightbulb moment – realizing we had the potential to solve a major problem in India, a country that has recently become a bio-manufacturing hub for the world.

We have all witnessed how India addressed the COVID-19 crisis by producing vaccines at scale, not only for itself but for the entire world. Interestingly, the production of these vaccines relies on precision fermentation technology. I was surprised to discover that some groundbreaking innovations, such as the production of animal-free insulin for diabetic patients and animal-free cheese using chymosin and vitamins, all use precision fermentation. This science is already a part of our daily lives, and that realization led me to think about removing animals from our food supply chain. This ultimately inspired us to become the first Asian startup focused on the future of food, starting with dairy proteins.

3. Can you recall an 'Only in India' challenge you faced and the innovative way in which you tackled it?

At first glance, India might not seem like the ideal place to build innovative companies in the deep-tech domain, which requires significant investments in R&D, longer timelines to launch products, the right government policies and, most importantly, patient capital to create an Intellectual Property (IP) driven sustainable business. Disruption using biotechnology or life sciences presents another challenge in India, as we don't see many emerging biotechnology companies that are recognized globally. On the other hand, India has the best science and engineering talent, low-cost bio-manufacturing capabilities that can produce at scale and, of course, one of the largest markets in the world.

Our experience has been a mix of all this, and we've tackled the various problems we confronted through a collaborative approach while working frugally out of India. For example, we've received multiple grants from the Indian government. At the same time, we've raised millions of dollars in funding, including from global climate tech funds like Green Frontier Capital. Whenever we faced an R&D infrastructure challenge in India, we looked at global startup incubation and acceleration programs to help us move closer to our goals. Overall, our experience has shown that India is one of the best places to create solutions to large global problems.

4. Imagine your startup as a character from Indian mythology. Who would it be, and why?

This is a tough but interesting question. If I had to choose, the first character that comes to mind is Lord Brahma. In Indian mythology, Brahma is known as the creator of everything. When we started Zero Cow Factory, we realized that there weren't many creators in this field, which opened up the potential for us to be one of the first companies to disrupt the $1-plus trillion dairy industry by removing animals from the entire food supply chain.

5. Which global company do you admire or draw inspiration from, and what aspects of its journey do you wish to emulate?

Some of the few companies we truly admire are tackling climate change, and most of them are based in the United States. I'd like to highlight some of the first disruptive startups in the cellular agriculture space, such as Impossible Foods (commercializing the first beef burger made without animals by using precision fermentation), GOOD Meat (commercializing the first cell-based chicken meat) and Perfect Day (commercializing the first whey protein using precision fermentation). These startups are pioneers in their fields, working as climate tech companies in the food-tech space, with valuations already reaching billions of dollars.

6. Paint us a picture of the opportunity landscape in India that your startup is tapping into. How big is this stage?

Considering biotechnology, India is the largest market. India is also emerging as a leading bio-manufacturing hub for the world, and we believe we're in the right place to work on the future of the bio-economy. The next century is expected to be defined by the bio-economy, and it's impossible to imagine this without India contributing to it on the world stage. India has proven to be the most conducive place for frugal innovation. This is what has allowed Zero Cow Factory to produce animal-free proteins at scale while remaining economically viable.

7. If your startup journey was a Bollywood movie, what would be its title and who would you cast as yourself?

Annam Brahma would be the name of the Bollywood movie about our journey as a startup. In Sanskrit and Hindi, the term means 'Food is God'. Our work at Zero Cow Factory is all about this, as we move towards the future of changing food. I want to play the lead character in this movie. My character's name would be 'Brahma' since I am the CEO of my company. In Hinduism, Lord Brahma is known as the creator of the universe. The movie would demonstrate the interconnectedness of the earth and food.

8. What myth about Indian climate startups would you bust with a fact or a story?

A common myth is that there aren't enough large climate tech funds investing in India. However, based on our experience in the climate tech space and having raised one of the highest seed rounds of $4 million in 2023 from prominent global and Indian venture capital firms, it's clear that if you're solving the right problem, global investors are ready to back you. We strongly believe India needs more investments to be made in climate startups, and we're already seeing this happen. Recently, Indian climate startups have scaled into big businesses across sectors like electric vehicles, agri-tech, food-tech, solar energy and green hydrogen technologies, raising millions of dollars from Indian and global VCs. India will experience a green revolution in the next twenty years, far beyond what we can imagine today. We can expect more foreign direct investment in this industry than ever before. The government is also taking significant initiatives towards a net-zero emissions mission, paving the way for a greener revolution in India compared to previous efforts in sustainability.

9. Describe a day in your life as a founder in India – the chaos, the calm and the caffeine.

A climate and deep research-led business has it all:

The chaos – when you're trying to solve a problem but aren't sure what will work in R&D. Your team comes up with different plans, and the chaos begins when you have limited resources to decide [which plan to adopt].

The calm – when one of your R&D plans actually works well.

The caffeine – when none of your plans work out, and you definitely need that shot of caffeine.

10. If you could have a cup of chai with an Indian (or global) environmental icon, who would it be and what would you ask him or her?

It would have to be Elon Musk. The founder of Tesla and other companies, he is a strong proponent of sustainability applied to the business world. That's why he invests in projects that use electricity from renewable sources. He even made Tesla Motors' patents public to encourage environmental protection and the fight against climate change, announcing that he would not oppose anyone using them in good faith to develop electric vehicles.

11. Which book, movie or figure in India has left a lasting mark on your entrepreneurial spirit?

I would say the movie *Swades*. The film revolves around the issues that development brings up at the grassroots level. The protagonist, a bright young scientist working as a project manager at NASA, returns to his village in India, which is diverse, vibrant and complex. The contrast between the highly developed world of NASA and his world back home in India is stark and leads him to a simple yet meaningful quest to generate electricity for his village. The film's 'We the People' tagline conveys that a country's strength lies in its people. Addressing numerous burning issues relevant today, *Swades* asks the vital question: 'As responsible and intelligent members of society, what can we do?' The film teaches us to stay connected with our roots and work for a better future – a lesson that entrepreneurs must never forget.

12. Fast-forward ten years – What's your vision of your startup's impact on India's climate action?

If you ask me to fast-forward to ten years later, I envision a reduction of at least 50 million metric tons of CO_2 equivalent, which means reducing the dependency on at least 50,000 cows to produce dairy products. It's massive, isn't it? Sounds crazy!

13. Ever received feedback from an Indian customer that made you go 'Wow'? Tell us!

Zero Cow Factory is such a cool name, isn't it? That's what we hear from everyone. As for customer feedback, we haven't had any from Indian customers yet, since we're still early in our market launch. However, many prospects are excited about what we're building. Most of them share our enthusiasm, as every organization today is focused on either net-zero goals or on adding more sustainable products to their portfolios. Cow milk without any cows would be an exciting reality soon – just like chicken meat made without killing any chickens or eggs created without the help of hens. Cellular agriculture is not only the future; it will become a necessity. Zero Cow Factory's animal-free casein could soon meet your expectations if you love cheese but wish to eat plant-based cheese!

14. Profit vs. planet – How does this debate shape your boardroom discussions?

We strongly believe that we don't have a Planet B. This means we have no right to damage our one and only Earth just to earn money. Prioritizing revenue at the expense of our planet will only create more problems for future generations. Earth has always provided for us, and it's our responsibility to protect it. Our boardroom discussions often revolve around this – if we can be profitable without harming the planet, then why not? It's about finding a balance where we can achieve both.

15. When pitching to VCs, what's the core story or angle you use to captivate their interest in your startup? Share with us your narrative, especially in the context of India's unique climate challenges and opportunities.

It is crucial to understand a VC's investment thesis. For example, pitching to investors focused on SaaS or unrelated domains won't be effective if you're building a climate startup. Targeting the right investment fund that is aligned with your problem or focusing on your business domain is important. As a climate startup, it's always better to pitch to climate or sustainability-focused funds and highlight the opportunity you have to address a significant problem, either within India or from India for the world. Emphasize the scale of the problem you're tackling, your business moat (with at least a 10x differentiation), the exit strategy for the investor and, most importantly, your impact metrics (like the reduction of carbon emissions over a certain period of time, as in our case).

16. For aspiring green entrepreneurs in India, what's your golden piece of advice?

India is poised to lead the world in the twenty-first century, and the coming years will undoubtedly be India's century.

The green opportunities emerging as we grow cannot be overlooked. Innovation and entrepreneurial capabilities arising from the net-zero ecosystem will drive impact and contribute to achieving our SDGs in India. Initiatives like 'Startup India' and various state government programmes underscore the increased political will to support this culture of entrepreneurship. Non-complex policies and sufficient funding are crucial for startups to grow and sustain. Entrepreneurs seeking capital to expand initiatives in sustainable development would strongly agree with this. Given the size of the Indian economy, the country is the third-largest emitter of greenhouse gases in the world, after China and the United States. Combating climate change is not just a trend but an urgent necessity that presents massive opportunities for new-age startups to drive a new green revolution in the country.

17. If you could wave a magic wand, what is one change that you would bring to the Indian climate tech ecosystem?

If one thing could transform the Indian climate tech ecosystem, it would be a progressive initiative from the Government of India regarding climate policies, subsidies, carbon credit incentives; every small measure [on their part] that could encourage the rapid adoption of sustainable practices. Government initiatives are crucial for climate tech startups to develop the ecosystem for the industry in the country, alongside large corporate houses receiving incentives for reducing every climate impacting activity. There needs to be a national mission for a greener India.

18. In your vision, what are two distinctly different but equally successful potential futures you see for your startup in the next five years?

First, if we can produce the same dairy experience in a lab as we do in traditional dairy production facilities but in a more sustainable way, then we absolutely should. Second, it's a significant win if that same product also protects our planet by reducing millions of CO_2 equivalents.

Conclusion

Zero Cow Factory is pioneering a new era in the dairy industry by demonstrating how we can enjoy cheese, one of our favourite foods, while simultaneously protecting the environment. This innovative venture is revolutionizing an industry that has historically posed environmental hazards, by employing precision fermentation technology. Zero Cow Factory's journey is a compelling example of how even the most formidable obstacles in the most traditional and sizeable of industries, such as the dairy industry, can be surmounted by the use of sophisticated technologies and forward thinking.

9

Log9 Materials's Bold Leap in Battery Innovation

After a fortuitous afternoon encounter over pizza with Akshay Singhal at a South Mumbai pizzeria, we were convinced that his story would occupy a truly unique place in *India's Green Startups*. Akshay's journey vividly illustrates what can unfold when a sharp scientific mind meets an unyielding commitment to climate change, and is a compelling example of how science and entrepreneurship can intersect to drive real, impactful change.

Akshay's story began during his time as a materials engineering student at IIT Roorkee, where he became fascinated with the potential of graphene and nanomaterials. This initial spark of interest eventually led him to found Log9 Materials, which is today one of India's most prominent climate startups that has become a leader in battery innovation, tailoring products to meet the unique conditions in India and other tropical regions. What really impressed us the most about Akshay was his ability to see the broader implications of his work and his focus on developing solutions that could address the specific challenges EVs faced in India's harsh climate.

Log9 Materials's research is innovative in addressing the fundamental issue of energy storage, which is essential for any country transitioning to a sustainable energy future. By creating batteries that can endure high temperatures and provide speedier charging times while maintaining consistent performance, Log9 Materials can potentially increase the viability of EVs in India. Log9 Materials's operations entail the use of deep-tech innovation, which is both a challenge and an opportunity; a challenge because of the lengthy gestation period of deep-tech projects, which necessitate continuous capital infusion, which may not always be available when most needed, and opportunity because, if successful, these projects can yield game-changing results.

Separately, Log9 Materials also has an asset management business, which is a service business that manages and optimizes the performance of battery assets used in EVs. It involves continuously monitoring battery health, predicting their lifespan and providing accurate information about battery performance and maintenance needs to all parties involved – like fleet operators and manufacturers. This ensures that batteries operate reliably, reducing the risk of unexpected failures and improving overall efficiency for fleets transitioning to EVs.

Akshay Singhal is pioneering a future where technology and environmental stewardship go hand-in-hand, offering hope and solutions in a world that desperately needs both.

1. How would you describe the climate problem your startup is solving in India?

Global energy demand for residential, industrial, mobility and agricultural needs accounts for over 70 per cent of carbon emissions. Cleaning up energy requires innovation in its generation, storage and transmission. We have set out to solve the storage challenge by disrupting the manufacture of batteries, deployment of solutions and management of their life cycle. India and the tropical world (the Global South) differ significantly from developed nations in the matter of operating conditions. High average temperatures, small vehicle platforms and distinct usage patterns stress lithium-ion batteries [in tropical countries]. Log9 Materials spearheads innovation across battery chemistry, pack electronics and management and AI-driven data analytics to enable the fastest charging, longest-lasting, highest-efficiency and safest batteries for commercial last-mile electric vehicles in India. With this, we target reduction of India's annual emissions by over 3 per cent by 2030.

2. Tell us a bit about yourself. What was the spark that ignited your startup idea? Share with us that lightbulb moment.

As a freshman at IIT Roorkee in materials engineering in 2011, I was fascinated with research. As I started to work in nanotechnology, I stumbled upon graphene as a new, upcoming wonder material. During my research internship at the University of Alberta in the summer of 2014, I grew bored with academic research. I decided to start a venture based on fundamental technological innovations in India. This gave birth to Log9 Materials in 2015 as a carbon nanomaterials venture, when I returned for my final year. After spending two years at the Technology Incubation and Entrepreneurship Development Society (TIDES) incubator of IITR as its first startup, we moved to Bengaluru, working towards potential applications of our carbon materials for climate solutions, which eventually led us to build batteries in India.

We quickly realized that the high tropical temperatures in India, our unique vehicle platforms (two- and three-wheelers and small, cost-effective four-wheelers) and usage patterns (shorter, more frequent trips) put immense stress on EV batteries. Against the functioning of the same batteries deployed across China, Europe and North America, in India we saw a reduction of 60 per cent in their life expectancy, along with severe loss of performance and high safety risk. Log9 Materials works on improving the chemistry of batteries for thermal resilience by enhancing the electrode and electrolyte formulations, cell design, platform-specific thermal management and precise characterization and analysis of cells throughout their life cycle.

3. Can you recall an 'Only in India' challenge you faced and the innovative way in which you tackled it?

Access to capital for deep-tech hardware ventures was tough to find. VCs would rather back Indian versions of proven startup models from the West or those that leveraged India's large consumer base, primarily selling the consumers stuff online that they would have previously bought from shops. So, hardly anyone would provide capital for research and innovation. Hence, we had to be frugal by leveraging whatever existing grant options were available, however small they were, and calling in favours with academic labs to get our samples tested at lower costs.

I still remember taking a grant to attend a research conference in Canada to get an opportunity to meet Dr Rudra Pratap, then director of the Centre for Nano Science and Engineering at IISc Bengaluru. He was also attending the conference as a speaker, and I had been unable to get an appointment with him before. I convinced the organizers to arrange a lunch meeting with him, which he agreed to. At the meeting I made a strong-enough impression that he offered us access to a $20 million-plus facility for just $1,000 a year. Later, over the years, we also got a cell fabrication laboratory set-up from Ather Energy (the largest electric scooter manufacturer, building fast and intelligent electric scooters in India) at a steep discount, leveraging the rapport I had built with Tarun Mehta, their founder, who believed we would make great use of the set-up for advancing battery cell technology development in India, which we did.

4. Imagine your startup as a character from Indian mythology. Who would it be, and why?

It would be Lord Vishnu. Vishnu is known as the preserver among the Trimurti – the triple deity of supreme divinity that includes Brahma and Shiva. In Vaishnavism, Vishnu is the supreme being who creates, protects and transforms the universe. Vishnu becomes an avatar (incarnation) to restore the cosmic order and protect dharma whenever the world is threatened with evil, chaos and destructive forces. Similarly, Log9 Materials is an avatar of Vishnu, here to create energy storage solutions that protect the climate, transform India's position on the world energy stage and restore climatic order.

5. Which global company do you admire or draw inspiration from, and what aspects of its journey do you wish to emulate?

Although I am a diehard Windows and Android user, I still admire how Apple has been built as a company. Their sheer focus on design and creating customer love is what I would like to emulate. Given the trends in the commercial EV sector in India, creating a holistic ecosystem of services that enable fleets to use their EVs most conveniently and efficiently generates the highest amount of customer love for them. This also provides insights for the constant improvement of designs and offers better products. While many would see Apple as a smartphone company, it's more of a design house and a smartphone ecosystem provider. So, product innovation combined with a focus on seamless customer experience is what I aim to replicate with Log9 Materials.

6. Paint us a picture of the opportunity landscape in India that your startup is tapping into. How big is this stage?

About 4,00,000 four-wheeler light commercial vehicle cargo vehicles, 4,00,000 three-wheeler high-speed passenger vehicles, 1,00,000 three-wheeler cargo vehicles, over 3,00,000 two-wheelers for deliveries and another 1,00,000 mid-size four-wheeler trucks are in operation in India. Given the rapid expansion of e-commerce and last-mile delivery services in India, these numbers will continue to grow rapidly, and all new sales of these vehicles are expected to be electric by 2030. This represents an overall market opportunity of more than $12.5 billion annually for electric commercial vehicle sales, with over $5 billion of this attributed to batteries. This could further expand by 50 per cent when we include buses, heavier trucks, industrial vehicles, boats and other means of transportation. An equally large opportunity lies with batteries for power backup and clean energy storage. Therefore, achieving over a billion dollars in sales by 2030 might be ambitious, but it is certainly possible for a leading battery player and commercial EV solutions provider.

7. If your startup journey was a Bollywood movie, what would be its title and who would you cast as yourself?

The Niners will showcase our team's relentless courage and conviction to solve India's climate challenges. This is true to the nature of the number 9, which, according to Indian numerology, is associated with courage, conviction and a strong desire to serve humanity. It embodies the spirit of perseverance and a commitment to overcoming challenges. I would cast Akshay Kumar for the role.

8. What myth about Indian climate startups would you bust with a fact or a story?

A common myth is that Indian climate startups will succeed primarily by creating application platforms or offering carbon accounting services and consulting based on technologies developed in the West. However, India's and the tropical world's climate challenges are quite distinct, and we need innovative local solutions tailored to our unique ecosystem to reduce emissions effectively. Energy demand is the biggest culprit, and since energy is a matter of national security, local innovations are critical.

It's not exactly a myth but an under-appreciated fact: India is the only major economy without a significant political divide on climate change. This has led to a stable policy environment supporting our journey towards net-zero emissions.

9. Describe a day in your life as a founder in India – the chaos, the calm and the caffeine.

My day starts with a rush to the gym, where my trainer always gives me looks for being late. I follow up on tasks, check morning emails and answer texts between sets of exercises. After a quick shower, I head to the office by 11 a.m., and have a late breakfast. I find that exercise gives me the necessary dopamine hit and mental peace for the day. Recently, I started creating a daily to-do list and following up on the previous day's tasks.

My workday involves attending meetings with the finance, manufacturing and product design teams and handling one or two investor pitches daily. If I get bad news, I take a walk, grab a coffee and call my co-founders, Kartik and Pankaj. If it's good news, I call them and we have tea together. I usually leave the office between 8 and 9 p.m., have dinner, make a few calls, watch TV, grab a drink with friends and then go to sleep. But this routine happens about fifteen to twenty days of the month, as the rest of the month involves extensive travel – late-night flights, hotel stays and trying to keep up with the gym while on the go. There are no complaints, whether it's meeting VCs, collaborators, climate founders or attending conferences. My wife says I begin to get irritable if I stay at home for more than ten days.

10. If you could have a cup of chai with an Indian (or global) environmental icon, who would it be and what would you ask him or her?

Well, I already did – and not just chai but a whole dinner – with Bill Gates. I asked him how he justifies having a steak and taking a private jet while being a climate activist and solutionist. The answer might seem too capitalistic for some, but it's hard to counter. He said he pays for the most premium carbon credits via carbon capture and storage (CSS) and other means – $300 million's worth of them annually. This offsets his footprint and enables new solutions to achieve scale.

11. Which book, movie or figure in India has left a lasting mark on your entrepreneurial spirit?

Mission over Mars, the story of India's orbital mission to Mars, left a lasting impact on my life. The teamwork, resilience, frugality and commitment to proving that we are no less than anyone is something every innovative startup could take inspiration from. A line that will always stay with me from that film is: 'India's dreams can never be matched with India's realities, yet what makes us win is that we hold our dreams dearer than our constraints.'

12. Fast-forward ten years – What's your vision of your startup's impact on India's climate action?

India's transportation sector accounts for over 10 per cent of the country's overall greenhouse gas (GHG) emissions. By leveraging our battery technology for mobility and clean energy storage, we strive to be leaders in cleaning up the country's commercial mobility segment. By enabling a holistic commercial EV ecosystem and providing it with access to 100 per cent clean energy for charging vehicles, we aspire to reduce 30 per cent of India's annual transportation-sector emissions, addressing 3 per cent of India's overall emissions.

13. Ever received feedback from an Indian customer that made you go 'Wow'? Tell us!

There have been many such cases, but I will highlight a few. Initial fleet customers who used three-wheelers powered by our batteries mentioned that with typical electric three-wheelers, they had to deviate from the most optimized delivery routes when delivering for Amazon. This was because, as the battery discharged, it couldn't carry the same payload, so they had to prioritize dropping off the heavier objects first. They were extremely happy that this issue was resolved with our batteries, which can deliver high currents at a lower charge state (lower voltage) to provide consistent power.

Similarly, we heard that fleets were moving away from EVs because the usual batteries failed even before the warranty period and replacements were unavailable. Severe operating conditions and more frequent fast charging led to premature battery failure, causing significant issues between financiers, fleets and OEMs. This made us realize that there was a need for better batteries and constant monitoring of battery health and performance, accurate assessment of their practical life and relaying of precise information to all stakeholders – leading to the birth of our asset management business, a service that manages and optimizes the performance of battery assets used in EVs.

14. Profit vs. planet – how does this debate shape your boardroom discussions?

While all investors on Log9 Materials's cap table invested knowing they were taking a climate tech bet, we, as humans, are naturally wired to lose sight of the long term. That's the fundamental problem with climate change. Its impacts are gradual and long term. Honestly, it's been a learning experience to see how quickly the agenda can get lost in discussions, and it's not always profit that blindsides it; often, it's market hype and short attention spans. For instance, we've had to repeatedly steer conversations away from targeting batteries for personal, consumer-oriented EVs. We constantly emphasize that if one aims to drive legitimate climate impact from EVs, they must have significantly high utilization, given the high upfront embodied emissions from the battery manufacturing process. Interestingly, this logic holds even from a cost-per-km perspective, as EVs are costlier upfront but have marginal running costs.

15. When pitching to VCs, what's the core story or angle you use to captivate their interest in your startup? Share with us your narrative, especially taking into account India's unique climate challenges and opportunities.

Our ability to work at the fundamental chemistry level of lithium-ion battery technology, understand it at the molecular level, innovate on it, fabricate the cells from basic materials and use that knowledge to manage them better at the battery-pack level is what puts us in a unique leadership position in the market. This capability has enabled us to assemble the largest battery R&D team in the country and provide the most advanced and high performance batteries available. This upstream-to-downstream control over all aspects of the technology gives VCs the confidence that we can consistently improve our products, stay ahead of the curve and still ensure maximized life, performance and safety under the harsh Indian operating conditions and constrained pricing expectations for our batteries.

16. For aspiring green entrepreneurs in India, what's your golden piece of advice?

The most important part of building a climate solution is to do it for the right reason and with a scientific approach. I meet so many so-called 'climatepreneurs' who are giving their venture a climate spin because that's the flavour of the season, or because they believe their solution has a positive climate impact because it feels so, intuitively speaking. Just because you use a naturally occurring biodegradable material for your product doesn't necessarily make it greener if the conversion process is quite energy consuming and cumbersome.

For example, I met a startup founder who had no clue about the carbon footprint of his bamboo range of products and was not even inclined to find out just because he was using bamboo. Please pursue your activity with the right intent and strive for the right data, no matter how contrary or scary it is. That's the only way you'll build a lasting solution. We don't have multiple chances to solve climate change anyway. It's here and now, and very quickly getting out of hand. Starting up is tough, and climate tech is even harder because you must chase money and impact. So, I would say, 'Don't do it for the glamour, please.'

17. If you could wave a magic wand, what one change would you bring to the Indian climate tech ecosystem?

I would create a $10 billion deep-tech hardware R&D grant scheme for startups managed by scientists and bureaucrats who have successfully commercialized innovations. Their teams would be incentivized to make the right decisions quickly by the companies having a VC-like carry structure linked to the success of the ventures they back.

18. In your vision, what are two distinctly different but equally successful potential futures you see for your startup in the next five years?

First, Log9 Materials could become a public listed company with an annual turnover of over $500 million, serving as a one-stop shop for all commercial electric vehicle needs – from battery to vehicle, financing, maintenance and 100 per cent clean charging, addressing over 1 per cent of India's annual emissions.

Second, Log9 Materials could be acquired by an international corporation as part of its decarbonization strategy, allowing it to own a large base of green assets consisting of mobility and stationary energy storage. This acquisition could generate average returns of 10x for our investors across multiple stages, and with the backing of the larger corporation, our tech stack could create an enormous climate impact.

Conclusion

Log9 Materials is rewriting the playbook on energy storage, proving that innovation doesn't only solve problems but, if done correctly, has the potential to reshape entire industries. This startup's relentless pursuit of better and more resilient battery technologies sets a new standard for what's possible in the world of clean energy. Their work is a powerful reminder that with the right blend of curiosity and commitment, more efficient solutions that meet today's challenges can be created to pave the way for a brighter and more sustainable tomorrow.

10

ElectricPe's Vision for India's EV Revolution

Beyond the transformative nature of ElectricPe's work, there are several other reasons why we felt we had to include Avinash Sharma, founder of the company, in our book. Apart from supporting the EV revolution in India, Avinash is redefining the role of green technology in the lives of millions of people. His startup journey combines vision, realism and social impact in a manner that would captivate climate-conscious individuals who are already oriented towards taking action on the issue.

Unreliable charging infrastructure is impeding the general acceptance of EVs in India, which is the very problem that ElectricPe seeks to solve. Thanks to government incentives and rules meant to lower pollution and cut oil imports, India is on the verge of experiencing an EV revolution. Given that their running costs are far cheaper than those of conventional cars, EVs are ideally suited for India's congested highways.

However, concerns about how far electric vehicles can travel on a single charge and the limited availability of charging stations have made many consumers hesitant to make the switch to EVs.

Given his background in the EV industry, technology development and business development, Avinash realized early on that producing stable and simple-to-use EVs and improving the overall ecosystem would be the key to rapid EV adoption in India. This is where ElectricPe's approach differs from those of other startups attempting to solve similar issues. With an app that allows users to identify and purchase an EV, charge and pay at any electric vehicle charging station, and access servicing and affordable battery subscriptions, ElectricPe, which calls itself the 'EV super app', is a real 'platform' business in that sense. As ElectricPe addresses national trust and convenience concerns, its primary focus is on providing dependable client experience.

Avinash Sharma's story is not just an account of entrepreneurial success but also a blueprint for others navigating the complexities of India's climate tech landscape. ElectricPe is an excellent example of how innovation can lead to transformative change when calibrated with a deep understanding of market dynamics and consumer behaviour.

This interview contains valuable insights into the mind of an entrepreneur who is as much a strategist as an innovator. Avinash's ability to see the broader picture is what makes his work at ElectricPe so impactful. Through ElectricPe, Avinash is addressing today's environmental challenges and setting the stage for a more sustainable and equitable future. In doing so, ElectricPe is not just contributing to India's EV revolution but leading it.

1. How would you describe the climate problem your startup is solving in India?

Many Indian cities have high pollution levels – we all know that. And the rising prices of petrol make it even worse. We are literally paying more to pollute more! That's where the EV becomes a no-brainer. It costs a tenth as much to drive and doesn't pollute. However, owning an EV is a whole different challenge. It's like solving one of the biggest brain teasers. First, you need to figure out how to charge it, given that there are various kinds of chargers (slow, fast, etc.). Then comes the problem of deciding which EV to buy. If you're purchasing a petrol scooter, you have fewer than ten brands to choose from. But with electric two-wheelers, there are currently over 250 brands! It's like picking a gadget like a mobile phone. You have your Apple and Samsung equivalents and a range of value-for-money brands. And finally, there's the headache of dealing with the battery. With a phone, one replaces it every two or three years when the battery degrades. But in India, we use our vehicles for much longer, especially since they cost much more than a phone.

We decided to do one thing – simplify! ElectricPe is India's only EV super app, a one-stop solution to all these problems. With the ElectricPe App, you can: (1) charge and pay at any EV charging point (like booking a table, dining and paying using Zomato), (2) buy any EV with custom guidance directly from the app (like home delivery of food or groceries through Zomato) and (3) purchase battery subscriptions that allow you to use the most updated batteries at any time without owning them (kind of like a LivPure RO where you don't own the RO system or its upkeep, and you pay for the water). All these facilities are in one app and available at the click of a button. This is how we are solving the brain teaser.

2. Tell us a bit about yourself. What was the spark that ignited your startup idea? Share with us that lightbulb moment.

I've spent over a decade working in sales, so I've spent most of my time outside the office, on the streets. Two things happened: (1) I developed a deep understanding of what buyers need and (2) I started noticing the things around me in my day-to-day life – who is selling what, who is buying what, etc. These two things became part of my DNA.

While driving daily, I noticed vehicles with green number plates (EVs in India have green number plate to distinguish them from regular vehicles). It was like noticing a 'glitch in the Matrix'. Over time, the number of these green-plate scooters overtaking me began to increase. At first it was just a minor observation, something I didn't pay much attention to, but it lingered in my mind. As the number of these 'glitches' grew, I thought to myself, 'Boss, something seems off. This is happening more and more.'

One day, while driving through Indiranagar in Bengaluru, it happened again. Without thinking, I honked at one of those scooters with a green number plate and asked the rider to stop. Naturally, he was irked and seemed ready to confront me, but I quickly apologized and asked him about the scooter he was riding. That's when everything began to unfold. He told me about his electric scooter and the improvisations he had made to deal with his charging struggles (he would carry the scooter into the lift to charge it at home!). Despite these challenges, he was happy with his purchase as it didn't pollute the environment and cost much less to drive. That was the Electric Spark! I realized that something big was happening – a huge wave of EVs was coming!

I started talking to every two-wheeler customer I could find, asking if they knew about EVs, their benefits and why they hadn't bought one yet. I personally spoke to about 450 people at malls, bus stands, tea stalls and other places. These 450 conversations led to what we now internally call ElectricPe's product roadmap.

Teaming up with Raghav Rohila, our chief product officer and an IIM-K alumnus with a rich background in product and operations, we formed a dynamic team. Our collective experience and shared passion for transforming India's mobility narrative fuelled the birth of ElectricPe.

3. Can you recall an 'Only in India' challenge you faced and the innovative way in which you tackled it?

This is a great question, because the 'Only in India' problem we stumbled upon created our strongest value proposition. Picture this: You drive into a petrol pump, and what's the first thing the person who dispenses fuel says before starting? '*Zero check kar lijiye, sir.*' (Sir, please check for zero). And most of us do check. We even stare at the display to ensure the requested quantity of fuel is pumped in. I bet you just remembered doing this yourself!

India is fundamentally a low-trust society. Now, with multiple charging stations coming up, each operating with its own app, the unique customer challenge is: Which app do I trust with my money? The same problem arises when choosing an EV – out of the more than 250 brands available in the market, which one can I trust to meet my specific needs?

We began solving for trust. The charging scenario is like a dining experience using Zomato (again, my favorite example). The restaurant you booked for a nice Friday dinner should exist when you arrive. It should be open, let you in, have the menu items shown on the app and accept payments via the same app so you can avail special discounts. In case of any issues, you shouldn't have to fight it out with the restaurant; you should be able to resolve them professionally and empathetically through the app (via reviews, complaints, etc.). Charging is similar – the charger should be physically available and functional, the billing should be accurate and the app should be able to handle complaints. The same goes for getting the right guidance to buy the EV that suits your needs, along with tailored financing, battery and servicing solutions – all to be taken care of in a trustworthy manner.

We chose to leverage machine learning to improve the service with every transaction, using data and deep tech to execute this on a large scale.

4. Imagine your startup as a character in an Indian mythology. Who would it be and why?

Definitely Arjun, the warrior prince. He was fighting a *dharma yuddha*, a righteous war. The Bhagavad Gita teaches us to imbibe qualities like gratitude, humility, forgiveness, love, care, affection and appreciation in our conduct. It emphasizes letting go of anger and ego, not allowing desires to overpower us and living a balanced life through all dualities – happiness and sadness, victory and defeat. It advocates working selflessly in the interest of others and always doing the right thing.

At ElectricPe, we've been fortunate to keep our focus on solving the climate problem while always putting the customer first and avoiding distractions. Our culture is rooted in working without ego, from believing that 'We don't know, so we will constantly seek the truth.' Of course, we make mistakes along the way, but we view them as learning opportunities rather than setbacks. Our goal is to earn customer love, and all our actions – whether to do with products, servicing or support – are geared towards this objective. We've operated with virtually no marketing budget, relying instead on doing the right things and working hard to see the results unfold.

The result? Our annual sales run rates have surpassed the capital we've raised, with almost zero-dollar marketing spend, most of our customers coming to us through word of mouth. The path to sustainability and profitability is incredibly fulfilling.

5. Which global company do you admire or draw inspiration from, and what aspects of its journey do you wish to emulate?

Two companies, actually. The first one is Netflix, for its people culture. I truly believe that a state, a nation or a country is made by its people, and so is an organization. Their famous book, *No Rules Rules*, clearly showcases the brilliance of Netflix's culture – their building a high density pool of talent, encouraging candour, providing freedom and accountability to everyone, working with trust and fostering ownership. Even if mistakes happen, those committing them aren't reprimanded; instead, the mistakes are treated as learning opportunities. We've embraced these cultural principles at ElectricPe from the start. There's even a dartboard in the office with the CEO's picture for people to throw darts at.

The second company is Tesla, simply because they made EVs mainstream. Tesla was a startup that disrupted the automotive industry, which was dominated by legacy players. They forced everyone to invest in EVs. Today, many major legacy automakers have decided to go fully electric – something unimaginable not long ago. Tesla achieved this by being ahead of the curve in customer experience and by using tech innovation as a differentiator. They've transformed the once-boring automobile into something more like a gadget with software updates, driverless cars and more. At ElectricPe, we always keep the customer at the centre of everything. We use deep tech and machine learning to create differentiation – not just for today but also with a vision of what the future will look like and what we need to build now to get there.

6. Paint us a picture of the opportunity landscape in India that your startup is tapping into. How big is this stage?

It's quite simple, actually. India has the world's largest population, young and aspiring. We are set to become the third largest economy in the world. Commuting is a basic human need – people travel to work, meet friends and family, etc. Today, a large portion of that commute happens using costly and polluting internal combustion engine (ICE) vehicles. As Indians, we intuitively understand the value of money and the effects of pollution (our country's capital is in the news every year for its pollution levels).

Imagine a future where all this commuting happens by EVs, and that day is coming soon! From a market-size perspective, India's EV market is set to touch $255 billion by 2030. The global EV market is estimated to rise to $1.5 trillion by the same time and Indian companies will be among the largest exporters too. There's much money to be made while building for a good cause.

Imagine this – soon, when we travel by road, there will be almost pin-drop silence (except for some chatter and a bit of honking here and there). Exciting, isn't it?

7. If your startup journey was a Bollywood movie, what would be its title and who would you cast as yourself?

If my startup journey were a Bollywood movie, its title would be *Itna Kaafi Nahi Hai!* (This Is Not Good Enough) since it embodies our core philosophy at ElectricPe: no matter what we achieve, we will always strive for more. Simple. It captures our relentless quest for excellence and our endless desire to break new ground, innovate and make a greater impact daily.

If I were producing this film, I would cast Rajkummar Rao as the lead actor. His unwavering commitment to creating meaningful and impactful work, characterized by extremely high standards of quality, resonates perfectly with the title *Itna Kaafi Nahi Hai!* The films he has starred in, such as *Newton*, *Stree*, *Kai Po Che* and *Shahid*, showcase his resolve to challenge himself, cross boundaries and deliver powerful messages. Like Rao, who is never satisfied and always seeks to improve further in everything he does, his portrayal of me in the film would symbolize our journey, which is centred on demanding more from ourselves to achieve greater societal impact.

This film will not only capture our ambition and resilience but also demonstrate that true success is measured by the positive change one can bring to society.

8. What myth about Indian climate startups would you bust with a fact or a story?

There's a lot of buzz around climate change and EVs right now. Everyone's talking about it and committing to the cause, including our government and the honourable prime minister. Most corporates, venture capital firms, fleets and e-commerce companies are also jumping on the climate bandwagon. The common belief is that by 2030, most vehicles in India must be electric. With all this excitement, whenever I tell someone that we're building in the climate EV space, they assume success is guaranteed since EVs are the future anyway.

That's the biggest myth. This future is a possibility that everyone wants to see happen, but what we're doing is working to solve the challenges that will turn that possibility into reality. And that's the tricky part. Why? Because convincing someone to buy an EV isn't just a product challenge – it's a habit-change challenge. We're used to buying a petrol scooter by default, knowing we can just drive into a petrol pump and keep moving. These are givens. But purchasing an EV means changing one's habits, which is hard. EVs are primarily charged at home, meaning no more petrol pump trips. EVs take longer to charge than petrol vehicles, which can be refuelled in minutes. And unlike a petrol scooter's fuel tank, an EV's battery degrades over time.

We've been used to buying and using petrol vehicles for over a hundred years. Changing those habits is tough, especially when they've become ingrained over a century. But then again, what's the fun in doing easy things? The effort required is directly proportional to the reward!

9. Describe a day in your life as a founder in India – the chaos, the calm and the caffeine.

Kab milegi khushi and a sense of achievement? (When will I get happiness and a sense of achievement?), I asked one of my investors. He congratulated me for our accomplishments, but I didn't feel elation. '*Nahin milegi*' (You won't get it), he replied, 'until you get used to it.' The constant pressure, the relentless pursuit of goals and the feeling that there's always more to achieve – it's a never-ending cycle that makes finding joy in the journey a challenge. That's the curse of being an entrepreneur.

An entrepreneur's life is full of nervousness, peppered with small, infrequent moments of joy. Eventually, you'll settle into the journey itself, and it becomes a way of life. There's always more to do, more to achieve, larger visions to build on, bigger dreams to dream – moments of unnerving calm and days of extreme chaos. That's when it hit me: the journey itself is the reward, at least for me. Real happiness and joy come when we add value – for our customers, the environment, country, colleagues and investors, who back us day and night.

10. If you could have a cup of chai with an Indian (or global) environmental icon, who would it be and what would you ask?

Sandiip Bhammer, for sure. Given the many things he handles, he's a difficult man to get a hold of (visit his profile online, and you'll see!). Despite this, his clarity, focus, dedication to climate action, institution-building, humility and energy levels never seem to dip. Every chat with Sandiip is sharp, insightful and enriching. And not just a cup of chai – that would last only a few minutes – I'd want to have a seven-course meal (even though I don't eat much) with him just to get more in-person time with him!

11. Which book, movie or figure in India has left a lasting mark on your entrepreneurial spirit?

India after Gandhi, for sure. Not for any political reasons, but because the book describes the monumental task of integrating and aligning all the states into one unified Bharat. It's a mind-boggling organizational challenge when you think about it. Every state, city and town is different in so many aspects. Getting everyone aligned under one grand vision requires extensive organizational efforts. Then the subsequent challenge is to bring this unified nation on to the international stage as a prominent player. I've learned a lot from this book and hope to apply at least some of those lessons as we build ElectricPe to last for a minimum of a hundred years!

12. Fast-forward ten years – What's your vision of your startup's impact on India's climate action?

We are very clear. If you're looking to buy a vehicle, consider an electric one. And if you do, buy it from us, we aim to be the one-stop shop, India's EV super app. Just as there's Swiggy/Zomato for food and Ola/Uber for cabs, there's ElectricPe for everything EV. That's our vision from a business perspective. At the country level, we want to lead the charge in climate action in India, creating a better, more affordable and sustainable future for its people.

We won't stop there, though. We're building electric mobility for the world, starting from India. We believe it's India's time to play centre stage on the global platform. We're clear that we want to lead this charge. India is one of the most diverse markets to cater to, and once we've achieved success here, we'll take the India EV stack to the world. Think of how UPI started in India and is now being adopted globally – that's exactly what we want to do with the EV stack.

13. Ever received feedback from an Indian customer that made you go 'Wow'? Tell us!

Absolutely! When we first started, our focus was on solving access to charging. Naturally, we hoped customers would use our platform to charge their vehicles. When the initial set of customers appeared, we were eager to speak with them. Something very interesting came out of those conversations. Someone said, 'Avinash, we were doing our evening walks and stumbled upon charging facilities in our society's common areas. We were already considering buying a scooter, and the moment we saw your charging facility, we decided to go electric since the charging issue was sorted.' This was our big Eureka moment. I thought, 'Wow! Our hypothesis is actually playing out in real life!' People bought EVs because they saw charging was available! I asked them more questions, and they said, 'Why don't you also provide EVs now that you already have a charging network that works well?' That insight led to our EV marketplace business model. Our entire product roadmap has been shaped by such customer feedback. All we did was to listen to them and implement their suggestions!

14. Profit vs. planet – How does this debate shape your boardroom discussions?

I'm quite clear on this. We are in the business of doing business. Our boardroom discussions always start with these questions: Are we solving a customer's problem? Are we doing it at least ten times better than everyone else? What impact are we creating? Once these questions are answered, we get down to the numbers. Profit pools are extremely important because they serve the objective of creating impact sustainably – meaning, on their own without relying on charity. A profitable business can continue to fuel expansion and create more impact.

15. When pitching to VCs, what's the core story or angle you use to captivate their interest in your startup? Share with us your narrative, especially in the context of India's unique climate challenges and opportunities.

I'm an operator-turned-entrepreneur. I spent over eleven years in various jobs, learning a lot along the way (and still do). I identified a clear opportunity that can create a massive impact and build a hugely profitable business. So, my core story or 'angle' is simply a set of facts, first principles and on-ground insights that indicate how the future will look. Simple.

16. For aspiring green entrepreneurs in India, what's your golden piece of advice?

Sustainable and profitable businesses take time to build. The journey is full of twists and turns as you search for the ultimate truths – product-market fit, moats, playbooks, go-to-market strategies, scale-up plans, etc. To build a legacy, a business that lasts a hundred-plus years, you need both patience to learn what works, why it works and how much customers are willing to pay, as well as an impatience to get things done quickly. Impatience helps you learn and execute faster, while patience ensures that results will come as long as you're doing the right things with undistracted focus day in and day out. Focus on the right inputs, and the right outputs will follow. Now, specifically for climate, the opportunity is right here. We're facing a human civilization survival challenge, which also means the opportunity is huge. I would encourage you to build the future.

17. If you could wave a magic wand, what one change would you bring to the Indian climate tech ecosystem?

If I had a magic wand, I would focus on 'upskilling'. Our educational courses are tailored more towards traditional industries like IT, electronics, civil and mechanical engineering. However, the huge climate opportunity of the future requires us to start building today. We need human resources with specific climate-related skill sets, whether it's in electric vehicles, sustainable farming, low-carbon construction materials or other areas. If I could, I would introduce multiple streams focused on the 'climate industry' in our undergraduate, graduate and postgraduate courses, and not just on the IT industry.

18. In your vision, what are two distinctly different but equally successful potential futures you see for your startup in the next five years?

We have a global vision, and time is the only variable at play. In the next five years, we could either be the market leaders in India, gearing up for global expansion, or we could already have scaled to select international markets, making significant inroads there too. The first scenario would involve establishing our dominance in India within the next two to three years, allowing us to expand globally sooner. The second scenario might take longer, but both paths are equally promising and successful.

Conclusion

By removing the main obstacles to EV adoption and making it more practical and convenient for a large number of Indians to transition to electric mobility, ElectricPe is a great example of how an innovative startup has the potential to alter India's clean-tech industry. The company's commitment to developing reliable and user-friendly charging infrastructure through its app will be essential in India's transition to sustainable mobility.

11

Newtrace's Green Hydrogen Revolution

When we were identifying startup founders in India to interview for *India's Green Startups*, we sought to spotlight those individuals and companies that were tackling climate change in unique and impactful ways. Among the myriad startups that we spoke to and met across India, some are attempting to achieve the impossible – redefining existing industries or, in some cases, creating entirely new ones. The Indian climate tech sector is clearly at a defining point, with its dynamic, young entrepreneurs innovating and challenging the status quo while addressing the complexities associated with climate change.

One such innovative and deep-tech-focused startup is Newtrace, which is committed to advancing a global green hydrogen revolution. Founded in 2020, Newtrace is currently at a product development stage. The company designs affordable and efficient electrolyzers that use renewable electricity to split water into hydrogen and oxygen, producing green hydrogen. This green hydrogen can be used as a sustainable energy source in various sectors, reducing reliance on fossil fuels.

Newtrace's electrolyzers are poised to support decarbonization across key industries, including heavy manufacturing, steel production, chemicals and refining, where green hydrogen can replace traditional carbon-intensive fuels. By targeting these sectors, Newtrace aims to play a crucial role in the global decarbonization movement, contributing to a cleaner energy future and supporting industry-wide shifts towards sustainability.When we first learned about Prasanta Sarkar, co-founder of Newtrace, we were immediately compelled to highlight his story. What drew us to Prasanta was not just the technology he and his co-founder, Rochan Sinha, were developing but the sheer resilience required on their part to bring such an idea to life in India's challenging climate tech landscape. The deep-tech arena is fraught with several obstacles, such as complicated regulatory frameworks and difficulty in accessing capital. This is a field that calls for a lot of patience and gobs of money. Yet, Prasanta and his team at Newtrace are navigating these challenges with a level of commitment that is both inspiring and necessary. They are pushing the boundaries of what's possible by working on developing advanced electrolyzers for green hydrogen production, which could play a critical role in decarbonizing industries. Their vision, courage, technical expertise and commitment to creating a more sustainable world are infectious. By combining extensive scientific knowledge with a mission-driven commitment to addressing the climate crisis, Prasanta and Rochan represent a new breed of Indian entrepreneurs. In a country where energy demands are soaring each year and the need for sustainable solutions is at an all-time high, their work goes beyond mere invention to shaping solutions that could change the world's environmental future.

Newtrace is more than simply a business because of the important role the company could play in the worldwide fight against climate change. Reshaping industries and considerably reducing greenhouse gas emissions could be achieved by developing cost-effective, scalable green hydrogen technologies. Prasanta's path – from rigorous academic research to becoming the founder of a cutting-edge enterprise – exemplifies the kind of game-changing work that is paving the way for a more environmentally friendly and sustainable India.

Through this interview you will understand the centrality of Prasanta Sarkar's experience to this book's narrative. His story mirrors not just the difficulties clean-tech businesses face in India, but also the tremendous potential that comes from the dedication of creative ideas to addressing the global climate crisis. Startups like Newtrace are leading the way towards a sustainable future for the planet. This interview encapsulates the imaginative and resilient attitude of the entrepreneurs who are powering India's climate tech boom.

1. How would you describe the climate problem your startup is solving in India?

The world needs a radical shift in its energy sources from fossil fuels to cleaner, alternative fuels. In most geographies around the world, including India, this energy transition journey is not only about fighting climate change but also about becoming energy independent and self-reliant. I believe that after '*roti, kapdaa aur makaan*' (food, clothing and shelter), the next frontiers are '*swaasthya* (healthcare) and *oorja* (energy)'. People with fair and equitable access to energy will always find ways to solve most of the challenges they confront. This is only possible by creating the technology infrastructure for energy transition and security.

At Newtrace, this is exactly what we aim to do. Newtrace enables the wide-scale adoption of affordable green hydrogen through our novel electrolyzer technology to help fight climate change and build a sustainable future for all. The world currently uses 100 million metric tons of hydrogen per annum (MMTPA) across refineries, fertilizers and chemical industries. The production of this hydrogen – primarily from natural gas and coal – is responsible for a billion tons of CO_2 emissions every year. With an increased focus on decarbonizing long-haul mobility, steel, cement, energy storage, etc., the demand for hydrogen is expected to rise to 230 MMTPA by 2030, and to 600 MMTPA by 2050. This is not sustainable with fossil fuel-based hydrogen production.

Electrolyzers are built on the idea of splitting water into hydrogen and oxygen using electricity from renewable sources. The current set of electrolyzer technologies has several bottlenecks in terms of raw materials, critical components, poor performance, high costs and supply-chain issues, which have halted their scaling up – something that is urgently required.

Newtrace develops electrolyzers that reduce the cost of producing green hydrogen as a result of its multipronged innovations across electrocatalysts and stack technology without dependence on rare earth elements, membranes and critical materials. These devices drastically improve performance, durability and reliability. We are building the industrial workhorse that will power future energy infrastructure, including renewable power storage and hydrogen refueling networks. Targeted industries for Newtrace's green hydrogen technology include heavy manufacturing, steel, chemicals and refining – sectors where green hydrogen can be a transformative alternative to traditional, carbon-intensive fuels. By enabling this sustainable shift, Newtrace aims to support the future of clean energy and industrial growth.

2. Tell us a bit about yourselves. What was the spark that ignited your startup idea? Share with us that lightbulb moment.

I grew up in Agartala. From an early age I was very passionate about becoming a pilot. This passion led me to a career in aerospace engineering, where I pursued my undergraduate and postgraduate degrees in India and the UK, respectively. I later worked with Leonardo Helicopters in Europe, designing modern rotor blades for helicopters. This experience led me to a research career at the Université Grenoble Alpes in France, where I earned my PhD, focusing on the growth and dynamics of cavitation bubbles, their damage potential and how they may be controlled and leveraged.

After completing my PhD, I decided to take a few months to backpack across India. I travelled from Kerala to Varanasi, and further to the Annapurna base camp in Nepal. During my journey, I witnessed first-hand how climate change affected lives and livelihoods in both urban and rural areas. The glaring challenges of access to energy were also very evident to me. This realization led me to decide to stay on in India and work on building the technology infrastructure necessary for fighting climate change and accelerating energy transition in the country.

3. Can you recall an 'Only in India' challenge you faced and the innovative way in which you tackled it?

My co-founder Rochan Sinha and I designed and developed our technology in my apartment in Indiranagar, Bengaluru. We wanted to build our proof-of-concept (PoC) technology demonstrator but had no dedicated space to do so. We couldn't ask potential investors to visit our apartment to see the PoC. We also weren't connected with any research labs in India and were unfamiliar with the research landscape, which typically involves a lengthy incubation process and bureaucratic paperwork.

We decided to do some research and identify key individuals who might take a chance on us and give us access to their labs and facilities. With perseverance and some luck, we eventually secured access to a leading research lab where we could build and demonstrate our PoC without the usual red tape. This access allowed us to develop our technology and added credibility to our work.

4. Imagine your startup as a character from Indian mythology. Who would it be, and why?

Interesting. Characteristically, I would say Newtrace has a lot of resemblance to Lord Shiva. We are associated with both destruction and creation via the destruction of fossil fuel-based energy systems and the creation of new energy infrastructure. Newtrace is creative, imaginative, fearless and fierce in its mission. We operate in some of the most difficult sectors and locations, accepting all contexts and requirements without differentiation. Our commitment drives us to reimagine and rebuild the future of energy.

5. Which global company do you admire or draw inspiration from, and what aspects of its journey do you wish to emulate?

I admire a lot of the work that has been done at Tesla from an organizational point of view. The intent to move fast, do the impossible, constantly innovate and cultivate a first principles approach is unique and enables everyone to build solutions to current and emerging problems. The ability to think like owners and the all-in team spirit drive alignment across the organization to collaborate and create something to improve the future.

6. Paint us a picture of the opportunity landscape in India that your startup is tapping into. How big is this stage?

India aims to produce green hydrogen at some of the lowest costs in the world and play a major role in the export markets, given its high renewable-energy resource endowment. Green hydrogen will enable the decarbonization of India's domestic industries, meet the growing energy demand and reduce energy import dependence, in line with its principle of self-reliance. The government of India targets at least 5 MMTPA of green hydrogen production by 2030. It has allocated ₹19,744 crores to meet this target, with the majority being provided as production subsidies for green hydrogen and electrolyzer manufacturers. This would also have an associated renewable-energy capacity addition of 125 GW, an investment of over ₹8,00,000 crore and the creation of over 6,00,000 jobs. This will cumulatively lead to a reduction in fossil fuel imports of over ₹1,00,000 crores and abatement of nearly 50 MMT of GHGs.

By 2030, the demand for hydrogen in India is anticipated to rise to 12 MMTPA from the current 5 MMTPA and, globally, to reach approximately 230 MMTPA from the current 100 MMTPA. This presents a massive opportunity to meet most of this demand through green hydrogen production in India.

7. If your startup journey was a Bollywood movie, what would be its title and who would you cast as yourself?

If our startup were a Bollywood movie, it would be called *Ek Nayi Raah* (A New Path) because that's exactly what Newtrace stands for. Newtrace signifies the creation of a new trajectory or approach in the fight against climate change and the pursuit of energy security, and in rethinking how we tackle these massive global challenges. We're charting a fresh path forward, using cutting-edge strategies, technologies and policies to create real, sustainable solutions that reduce carbon emissions, manage energy resources and protect our planet for future generations.

Who better to play the lead role than Akshay Kumar? He's got the versatility, passion for real-life stories and transformative ability to embody what Newtrace stands for truly. Akshay's strong screen presence and connection to socially relevant themes make him the perfect fit to bring our journey to the big screen. Plus, his box office appeal would ensure our message reaches and inspires a wide audience. We're ready to show the world what Newtrace is all about!

8. What myth about Indian climate startups would you bust with a fact or a story?

I think, for most of the time, the Indian climate startup ecosystem was assumed to be focused mainly on the mobility sector. Even when we started, green hydrogen was directly compared with electric mobility and the advantages/

disadvantages of both. Decarbonization and electrification had become synonymous, and it took us quite some time and effort to educate startups and VCs about what we were doing differently. Now we are seeing more and more startups coming to the forefront with innovative solutions for decarbonizing 'hard-to-abate' industries and sectors, including mobility, and the wider world is recognizing this too.

9. Describe a day in your life as a founder in India – the chaos, the calm and the caffeine.

The day begins early with a cup of freshly brewed coffee and planning for what's ahead. As the founder of my company, my schedule is usually packed with meetings involving both internal and external stakeholders. Early planning helps me think through the expected outcomes and actions needed to make my sessions as productive as possible. Preparation usually starts the night before. The routine starts at the office with another cup of coffee and a quick check-in with my co-founder Rochan. I like spending the morning focusing on my tasks and catching up on emails.

After that, I dive into scheduled meetings and project reviews, squeezing in a quick lunch somewhere in between. Whenever possible, I try to have lunch with Rochan and most of the team. The day continues with customer discussions, investor pitches, team meetings and more project reviews, often fuelled by coffee.

Once back home, I wind down with dinner, some Netflix and a walk. Before bed, I prepare for the next day or read, depending on the agenda.

10. If you could have a cup of chai with an Indian (or global) environmental icon, who would it be and what would you ask him or her?

I'm particularly curious about meeting figures like Tulasi Gowda, known as the 'encyclopedia of the forest' in India. She was awarded the Padma Shri in 2020 for her contributions to environmental conservation. She has an incredible wealth of knowledge about various plant and herb species, having planted and nurtured thousands of trees since she was twelve years old. I would love to walk through the forest with her, learning about the different species and their unique characteristics. Another inspiring figure is Jadav Molai Payeng, known as the 'forest man of India', who dedicated thirty years of his life to creating a forest and restoring wildlife on a river island.

11. Which book, movie or figure in India has left a lasting mark on your entrepreneurial spirit?

The Almanack of Naval Ravikant has had a lasting impact on my entrepreneurial journey. Naval Ravikant's philosophies emphasize the importance of long-term thinking, leveraging unique insights and prioritizing personal well-being, all of which are critical elements in the challenging journey of building a transformative business in a complex field like green hydrogen.

12. Fast-forward ten years – What's your vision of your startup's impact on India's climate action?

By providing carbon-neutral alternatives to various industries, we pave the way for a healthier and more sustainable future for humanity and the planet. Newtrace is dedicated to developing the technological infrastructure necessary to make hydrogen the mainstream energy source in all industry sectors. We focus on tackling the most challenging problems across industries and in creating advanced infrastructure to facilitate a sustainable energy transition to hydrogen. We recognize the potential of hydrogen in reducing carbon emissions in 'hard-to-abate' sectors, and we aim to catalyse significant transformation for them.

Our ultimate goal is to drive global decarbonization through innovative solutions, and affordable green hydrogen production technology is just one of the many challenges we intend to address. In ten years, our activities will span the 'molecule to energy' business, providing carbon-neutral technology alternatives across all industries, which would lead to the abatement of many hundreds of millions of tons of GHGs.

13. Ever received feedback from an Indian customer that made you go 'Wow'? Tell us!

Yes, absolutely. In our last deployment, our customers were extremely pleased with the hydrogen purity produced by our system. The product quality and performance were on par with the best in the world for such a complex product, and our customers were amazed that we could achieve that so early on in our journey. Other feedback received from customers is about the impressive quality of our team in terms of their capabilities, their understanding of the problem (we are trying to address), the technology space and our intent to solve problems and add value.

14. Profit vs. planet – How does this debate shape your boardroom discussions?

Profit and planet are both core parts of what Newtrace is doing. While the planet guides our choices, actions and the problems we choose to solve, it is imperative to build a sustainable business to have the biggest impact. We are driven by the current climate challenges and the urgency to address them now, not a decade later. Climate challenges are vast and dynamic in nature, so it is important that we continue to iterate, innovate and invest in capabilities to tackle these evolving challenges. We remain focused on strong business fundamentals to enable us to address both short-term and long-term difficulties effectively.

15. When pitching to VCs, what's the core story or angle you use to captivate their interest in your startup? Share with us your narrative, especially in the context of India's unique climate challenges and opportunities.

When pitching to VCs, we always start by sharing the personal journeys of the founders and our team, highlighting how our diverse experiences have enabled and motivated us to build Newtrace. We then weave in the problem statement, outlining what has been accomplished so far and how we are uniquely positioned to seize this significant opportunity across sectors. We focus on how we are among the few startups offering this particular solution globally, and emphasize our key differentiators and the global impact of our company's success.

16. For aspiring green entrepreneurs in India, what's your golden piece of advice?

Solve the harder problems! The more difficult the problem statement, the greater the impact and reward. Success might not be immediate but, on a long-term horizon, solving the harder problems builds a strong moat around your business.

17. If you could wave a magic wand, what one change would you bring to the Indian climate tech ecosystem?

Honestly, I would like to see more action on the ground towards supporting innovation and technology development across climate tech. We have an uphill task regarding the quantum of challenges and the pace at which they must be addressed. The time to act is now, not a decade later. There has to be more support for early-stage innovative solutions for building technologies and demonstration, and for increased capital availability, specifically for growth-stage company building and for facilitating industry collaboration for early action.

18. In your vision, what are two distinctly different but equally successful potential futures you see for your startup in the next five years?

In the long run, Newtrace could evolve into an energy company that spans technology development, project execution, green chemicals production and energy and carbon-credits trading. Another possibility is to build Newtrace into a product and software design company focused on developing and licensing technologies across sectors. We are committed to traversing difficult paths to fulfil our vision of decarbonizing the world through innovation. Our goal is to build an enduring company where, at each stage, we will strive to maximize value for all our customers, stakeholders and partners.

Conclusion

Newtrace is a shining example of what Indian innovation can achieve in the clean-tech sector. Its unwavering commitment to making green hydrogen both accessible and affordable is set to revolutionize industries in search of sustainable energy solutions. By continually pushing the boundaries of what's possible, Newtrace is redefining how technology can be leveraged to tackle the pressing climate challenges of our time. As it forges ahead, Newtrace is setting new benchmarks in the industry and inspiring the next generation to pursue ambitious and sustainable solutions that will shape a greener future for the country and the planet.

12

Zerocircle's Seaweed-Powered Solution to Plastic Pollution

Neha Jain conveys a powerful, modern and transformative story through her unique startup, Zerocircle. As a visionary founder, she has transformed her personal dissatisfaction with the state of the environment into a project capable of delivering global impact. 'Grit' and 'dedication' are the two words that come to mind when one thinks of Neha's impact on lasting and meaningful innovation.

Neha's route to sustainability was not straightforward. She began her career in technology at Google, far from the environmental issues that would eventually define her work. However, her daily experiences in Mumbai, such as the sight of plastic waste covering the beaches and hazardous odours billowing from nearby dumping grounds began bothering her. They were daily unpleasant reminders of the expanding trash problem in the city, which appeared to have no end in sight. For the problem-solving Neha, these everyday encounters proved impossible to avoid and eventually compelled her to reconsider her career path, leading her to leave the technology industry to pursue a cause that felt far more urgent and meaningful.

Zerocircle was born from Neha's desire to create a tangible, sustainable solution to the pollution crisis. What sets Zerocircle apart is its focus on seaweed – a resource that is usually overlooked but which Neha recognized for its incredible potential. What sets it apart from other crops is that it does not require freshwater, land or fertilizer to grow, making it extremely resource efficient. Since 2020, Neha and her team at Zerocircle have been working on creating viable eco-friendly substitutes using seaweed for single-use plastic, including packaging materials and disposable items. If successful at a commercial scale, it will help tackle environmental issues while providing economic support to coastal communities, which can then cultivate seaweed for their livelihood. Several companies and manufacturers are working closely with Zerocircle to move away from traditional plastic packaging alternatives and opt for Zerocircle's sustainable alternatives, marking a significant shift towards more responsible production practices.

It hasn't been smooth sailing for Zerocircle. Developing a product that can replace single-use plastic products on a large scale and be produced affordably and efficiently has posed numerous difficulties. Neha has faced challenges with scaling production to meet high demand, ensuring the durability of seaweed-based materials in various climates and securing a reliable supply chain for consistent seaweed sourcing. Additionally, achieving competitive pricing has been difficult, as eco-friendly alternatives often face higher production costs than traditional plastics. Neha understands that true sustainability involves a product's entire life cycle to benefit both people and the planet. This commitment to 'holistic' sustainability is what propels Zerocircle, even when the hurdles appear insurmountable.

Neha stands out for her ability to mix empathy with invention. She is establishing a movement redefining our interaction with the surroundings, and not just a product. Her efforts at Zerocircle illustrate how entrepreneurship can be used to do good while creatively and inclusively addressing some of the planet's most urgent problems.

For readers of *India's Green Startups*, Neha Jain's narrative serves as a beacon of what can be achieved when passion, purpose and innovation intersect. Zerocircle is no ordinary startup – it's shaping our future by taking single-use plastic head on, and that too by using one of nature's most versatile resources. Neha's path presents hope and a roadmap for the transformation we all wish to see on a planet sorely in need of answers.

1. How would you describe the climate problem your startup is solving in India?

I think the importance of clean air for India, where cities often exceed 400 in the air quality index (AQI), hardly needs to be explained. While our forests play an important role in drawing down carbon, it's important to know that 50 per cent of oxygen on the earth comes from the oceans. India enjoys a long coastline along which thirteen of its high-value states and union territories are located. As much as we gain from the oceans, we become highly vulnerable when we disrupt our ocean cycles. However, any damage to this ecosystem is often isolated and diagnosed symptomatically. The thin film of plastic that chokes rivers and city sewage is isolated as a water pollution problem affecting aquatic and marine species. We often forget that water connects rivers with oceans and countries with continents. A grocery bag discarded at Miami Beach can end up at Mumbai Chowpatty, and vice-versa.

The degradation mechanism of biodegradable plastic is only tested and certified for soil, while India happens to be one of the biggest contributors to oceanic plastics. Microplastics caused by non-degradable materials aren't just a landfill problem. It is also not just a problem linked to its source – petroleum. These microplastics that float as debris in our oceans disrupt the biological function that allows upper-sea creatures to convert carbon dioxide into oxygen. If left unchecked, they can break the cycle of life in the sea, jeopardizing our existence. Unfortunately, our current statistical system and narrow life cycle analysis can't measure this impact on the planet or on our country. That's the problem we strive to solve for our country and the world; we are solving a local problem with a global solution.

2. Tell us a bit about yourself. What was the spark that ignited your startup idea? Share with us that lightbulb moment.

I spent several years working with Google, but the excitement of building digital tech solutions dissipated when I was confronted with the realities of my living world. I distinctly remember a dump that was a few kilometres away from my house. It would catch fire occasionally, leaking toxic gases into the city of Mumbai. Somehow, that news affected me a lot. I would frantically segregate my waste, compost my leftovers and buy less, but the mountains of waste wouldn't change. During beach cleanups, I noticed millions of microplastic particles in the sand. I refused to give away the plastic waste from my home because I was convinced I could find a suitable recycler somewhere. Over eight months straight, this refuse had become the size of a room in my apartment in Mumbai.

After leaving the tech sector, I started consulting on sustainability-related projects. And I finally landed a project to solve some of the problems of the landfill. Two things became increasingly clear: fast-used materials like plastics must be made of natural chemistry and from resources that don't hurt the planet. Agricultural products like sugarcane and corn didn't fare well on resource efficiency, like their use of land and water, or competed directly with our food. One day, I found the answer in the ocean.

The ocean covers 70 per cent of the planet, and 97 per cent of the world's seaweed grows around us. Seaweed doesn't require freshwater, land or even fertilizer. It keeps the ocean cool and grows sustainably on farms. With the help of a prominent marine biologist, I learned that it was possible to build a science that could convert seaweed into a replacement for the all-pervasive flexible plastics. It wasn't merely an opportunity but an invitation to anyone listening to do something about it.

3. Can you recall an 'Only in India' challenge you faced and the innovative way in which you tackled it?

I'd probably coin it as an 'Only in India' opportunity. While the seaweed industry is still budding in India, our proximity to the heart of the global seaweed hub (China, Indonesia and the Philippines), where 97 per cent of the world's seaweed is cultivated, presents a remarkable advantage. As the world wakes up to its incredible benefits, there has been a rising demand for raw materials worldwide. What's intriguing is that Southeast Asian markets lack the advanced infrastructure to produce value-added products at scale to maximize returns for growers. Since the import duty on these raw materials is low, it makes logical sense for refineries and downstream players in India to rely on imports to begin with, and they did.

Our goal was to take advantage of this opportunity strategically and sustainably. We've forged a strategic partnership with one of the world's leading bio-stimulant and fertilizer companies to achieve vertical integration. This means 85–90 per cent of wet biomass can go into their production, and the rest (compounds of interest) get passed on to us. These mutually exclusive compounds help us manage the pricing fluctuation resulting from supply and demand factors in India. In terms of environmental stewardship, our approach alleviates the pressure on existing farm owners to scale their operations exponentially year after year.

4. Imagine your startup as a character from Indian mythology. Who would it be, and why?

If I recall mythological stories from my childhood correctly, I would pick Vishvakarma for his craftsmanship. In the modern world he would represent our chemists and engineers. I would then pick the symbolism of Parvati's nurturing and all-giving nature, which seamlessly ties in with our regenerative material – seaweed. Finally, I'd pick the attitude and spirit of the *vaanar sena*, who brought down invincible forces, much like our fight against big oil.

5. Which global company do you admire or draw inspiration from, and what aspects of its journey do you wish to emulate?

There are quite a few companies that I find admirable in the way they operate. Patagonia is obvious for its pioneering work with sustainable materials, environmental activism and an unconventional spin on capitalism. However, my personal favourite is Burton. They specialize in outdoor sports gear and is loved by snowboarders worldwide. They have been a leader in design and innovation, which is evident across all their departments. When collaborating with innovators, their discussions extend beyond the ordinary. They're not afraid to take early risks and tackle challenges others haven't dared to attempt. I would love to emulate this culture as we grow, so every individual associated with us becomes the brand custodian of what we represent.

6. Paint us a picture of the opportunity landscape in India that your startup is tapping into. How big is this stage?

Our plastic alternatives are designed to break down naturally and biologically in any mismanaged environment, be it soil, landfill, oceans or even inside the human body – effectively eliminating microplastics right from the source. Our materials have been tested in a simulated whale gut, proving not only to be marine-safe but also safe for marine life.

This innovation presents a significant market opportunity, representing the potential to replace 180 billion polybags within the fashion industry where most products are manufactured in India and its surrounding regions and shipped to global markets like Europe and North America. There also exists an opportunity in replacing every plastic-coated food delivery box carrying your burgers, pizzas and biryanis with our coating, and finally making our lunches and dinners healthier and microplastics-free. Our drop-in solutions are purchased not by brands but by the plastics manufacturers and converters of brands. India ranks among the largest producers in the plastics industry in Asia, with roughly 30,000 processing units. This solution is designed for them. If you look at the potential scale of use of the raw material, the opportunity for India is 7,500 kilometres of seaweed farming, with women forming the majority of the workforce. By providing sustainable packaging solutions, we aim to make a meaningful impact on both environmental preservation and industry practices.

7. If your startup journey was a Bollywood movie, what would be its title and who would you cast as yourself?

I'd tweak an existing film title instead of picking a new one. *Kal, Aaj aur Kelp* would be a movie depicting the future. As we unwrap what lies ahead, nature-inspired solutions will play a pivotal role in the world, learning from and mimicking the elegance of natural systems. Another title that comes to mind is *Jab Sally Met Algae*. It would be the story of a woman discovering seaweed and falling in love with it. My journey isn't very different. I have travelled along the entire coast of Maharashtra with a leading Indian marine biologist looking for seaweed. The insights I gained convinced me that there is much more to this journey than just starting a business. It is also about empowering an entire coastal community. I would like Sanya Malhotra of *Dangal* fame to play my role – a strong woman character who is real and not plastic-painted.

8. What myth about Indian climate startups would you bust with a fact or a story?

It's a common misconception that innovation and technology are more evolved in the West. While they certainly receive a healthy amount of funding and attention, it's important to recognize the unique strengths of Indian climate startups.

In India, we have abundant biomass, robust manufacturing capabilities and access to valuable resources, giving us an edge in the biomaterials industry. We stand apart because of our ability to develop solutions tailored to our region's specific challenges and climatic conditions. For example, while colder countries may focus on solutions that withstand extreme cold or snow, our solutions are tested for harsh conditions like intense heat, humidity and the monsoons. I believe contextually appropriate solutions and local expertise should be the primary benchmark for technology evaluation.

9. Describe a day in your life as a founder in India – the chaos, the calm and the caffeine.

Every morning, before I'm fully awake, my cat's soft, calm meow serves as my alarm clock – one with no snooze, just razor-sharp consequences if I do not wake up. I reach for the most prized possession of the day: my cup of tea. That's when I remind myself to breathe deeply, knowing the day will rarely follow what my calendar promises.

As the next hour unfolds, tasks pile up: accounting reviews, inquiries from major Consumer Packaged Goods (CPG) brands, scheduling sample shipments, tracking production timelines, negotiating fundraising with investors, interview requests, international submission deadlines, hiring pipelines, R&D updates, certification finalizations, regulatory approvals and budgeting for events and travel. Each demands more attention than the other, prompting me to reach for my second cup.

I then start dividing tasks based on their priority, respond to emails systematically and snooze them for a re-look from a comfortable distance in time. By 9 a.m., I tell myself I've conquered most of the day, but that's just my way of saying I've made it through the first wave of chaos. Now, my phone is off the hook. On my way to work, I tackle another round of tasks with the most active external agencies at this time of day. I walk into the office and head straight to the lab, where I enjoy my little chit-chat with our team of chemists, figuring out why something that wasn't working is now working, or vice versa. But they always hit me with a statistical rundown of the situation, nudging me to read more and call for another round of discussions to play the devil's advocate on our positive findings.

Around noon, as my conversations turn to strategic planning, someone from the production team always seems to deliver news about a malfunctioning machine part or a delayed delivery from a supplier. My discussions swing from million-dollar targets to troubleshooting electrical issues and jammed shutter motors. There's always something new every day.

As Zerocircle's official hours wrap up, investors call for updates on the funding round and mentors share their advice. So much so that on my way home, I've even been offered investment opportunities by three Uber drivers, which I graciously thank them for and ask them to spread the word. On a good day, if I don't have any late-night calls with overseas associates and clients, I unwind with my family and my four cats and watch a detective TV series. My cats purr on my cheeks, helping me drift into a perfect eight-hour sleep.

10. If you could have a cup of chai with an Indian (or global) environmental icon, who would it be and what would you ask?

Undoubtedly, it would be Sylvia Earle, also known as 'Her Deepness'. I'm a big fan. I've had the fortune of listening to her up close at the World Ocean Summit in Lisbon, but not the opportunity for that cup of tea with her. In a world where the ocean often remains 'out of sight, out of mind' for many, her lifelong dedication to ocean conservation is truly remarkable. While it may be the millionth retelling of her encounter with the humpback whale, I'd love to hear about her surreal experience when a majestic humpback whale looked back at her with equal curiosity, its large eyes fixated on her, circling around her as she floated on the surface during her expedition. Given her profound understanding of the ocean's ecosystems, I would seek her insights on how material innovators can leverage the ocean's resources responsibly and ethically to scale sustainably.

11. Which book, movie or figure in India has left a lasting mark on your entrepreneurial spirit?

I would say *Chillar Party*. It's a fun, carefree and heartwarming story of a gang of kids who take on a big-shot politician in their neighborhood because they believe fiercely in their cause. And what's their cause? Saving a stray dog! It's a simple yet fantastic story of the underdog that resonated greatly with me. The movie really hits home on teamwork and the power of coming together.

In 2020, when I started Zerocircle and the team started coming together, none of us had experience with biomaterials, but there was this shared excitement to create something together. We had just begun, and there was no promise of success, which is a mark of entrepreneurial spirit. Despite being little, these kids band together to stand up to this big, self-centred villain. What struck a chord with me personally were the themes of caring for animals, friendship and standing your ground when the going gets tough.

12. Fast-forward ten years – What's your vision of your startup's impact on India's climate action?

I imagine our technology would have seamlessly integrated into India's industrial landscape fabric. The supply chain for our biomaterials would have undergone a monumental shift. What was once a fragmented and experimental ecosystem would have evolved into a well-oiled machine. Suppliers, manufacturers, distributors and brands would seamlessly collaborate within a stable marketplace, ensuring efficient production and distribution of biomaterials. Businesses across multiple industries would reap the rewards of higher efficiency, cost savings and enhanced brand reputation by incorporating our materials into their products. Stringent regulations would be in place to incentivize the adoption of sustainable materials while discouraging greenwashing practices. Carbon and plastics tax benefits would provide powerful incentives for businesses to embrace our solution. Our impact would extend beyond national boundaries, we would emerge as global frontrunners in sustainable materials.

13. Ever received feedback from an Indian customer that made you go 'Wow'? Tell us!

This question takes me back to our first coating trial in Maharashtra when we wanted to check how compatible our greaseproof coating (for the food takeaway and delivery industry) was with the existing infrastructure. These trials show us the reality of our materials, and it's good to get a reality check early on. While the converter gave us rave reviews, the 'wow' moment came when he turned around mid-test and told us that our product provided an excellent grease and oil barrier and enhanced the printability of the paper, an application highly relevant for the packaging market. You can imagine the joy when a customer discovers a unique benefit of your product that you didn't necessarily design it for. Before the day ended, he placed a large order for his customers in the UAE. That moment made us realize we had barely scratched the surface with this material and were just starting.

14. Profit vs. planet – How does this debate shape your boardroom discussions?

Interestingly, before it reaches profitability, it often starts with chemistry. There are no known ways of scaling up production of natural polymers using existing infrastructure. We are at the forefront of solving this science. More often than not, the debate is about whether we can mix some easy elements (read not-so-sustainable but significantly better than incumbents) into our materials to ease the process. Of course, it'll come as no surprise that several large brands have suggested this upfront. Large corporations usually solve such problems by saying they sell oat biscuits but really sell maida products. While our conversations veer off in many directions, the final decision always favours the ocean. The harder path is what we decide on as a team. We can leave behind all the good-to-haves, but not what we stand for.

15. When pitching to VCs, what's the core story or angle you use to captivate their interest in your startup? Share with us your narrative, especially in the context of India's unique climate challenges and opportunities.

When pitching to VCs, I focus on telling a story that intertwines environmental responsibility with strong commercial potential. At Zerocircle, we're not simply another packaging company. We are a biotech enterprise committed to harnessing natural and regenerative resources. This isn't just about creating materials, but about redefining how we interact with the environment.

Seaweed is a prime example of this. Often known only as a sushi wrap, it has untapped potential. When I share the journey of seaweed being cultivated in Tamil Nadu, Gujarat or Maharashtra and transformed into a material mimicking plastic without any harmful effects, it captures attention and opens up a conversation. Next, we delve into the technology that makes this transformation possible. Our team of Indian scientists, chemists and engineers worked tirelessly to develop and patent the technology that allows us to produce this material at scale. This achievement, accomplished in just two years, isn't just a testament to our innovation but also to our readiness to scale – a critical point for investors who are as concerned with feasibility as they are with vision. From here, the conversation naturally shifts to the commercial viability of Zerocircle. The fact that 97 per cent of global seaweed farming happens in Asia – a region that also leads in both production of plastic packaging and oceanic plastic waste – puts us at a unique intersection of problem and solution. This geographical and economic convergence allows us to influence pricing on a global scale while maintaining competitive costs, a compelling proposition for any investor.

What truly sets Zerocircle apart is the broader socio-economic impact we are poised to make. The communities farming seaweed, the brands choosing sustainable materials, the manufacturers collaborating to bring these products to market, the consumers using our goods, and even the recyclers and waste managers – each of these groups benefits from the ripple effect of our innovation. And beyond the business metrics, there's the undeniable impact of our activity on the environment, both on land and in the oceans. By offering a real alternative to plastic, we enable investors to make a significant positive difference across multiple sectors.

For me, this journey is deeply personal. Zerocircle isn't just a company; it's part of my life story. It's the story of people working to make a change, the story of stray animals who deserve a world free from plastic waste, the story of Indian fishing communities creating sustainable livelihoods. And yes, it's the story of my cats, who inspire me to keep pushing forward. Ultimately, Zerocircle is about hope and the future we can build together – a future that aligns profit with purpose in a meaningful and impactful way.

16. For aspiring green entrepreneurs in India, what's your golden piece of advice?

My golden (or green or blue) piece of advice is this: When building a climate-resilient solution, ensure that every detail is connected, even those often overlooked or conveniently omitted. Remember, you're moving into uncharted territory, so have faith in your solution. Collaborate with fellow solutionists because what's ahead is much bigger than what one lonely whale can swallow.

17. If you could wave a magic wand, what one change would you bring to the Indian climate tech ecosystem?

If I could, I would change the mindset around short-term gains. Unlike digital platforms and the SaaS industry, climate tech operates on a completely different level. Scale in this context depends on physical infrastructure, which requires substantial real-world support. There's a significant need for hard capex investment in these technologies, which young startups, especially in their early stages, often can't afford hence they take on on debt till they reach a certain level of revenue generation. The market demands rapid commercialization, clients expect affordability and investors anticipate fast exits. By changing this mindset, we can create an environment prioritizing long-term sustainability and resilience in addressing climate challenges.

18. In your vision, what are two distinctly different but equally successful potential futures you see for your startup in the next five years?

In one potential future, Zerocircle becomes a leader in the sustainable materials industry by scaling its eco-friendly packaging solutions across a wide range of sectors. Imagine Zerocircle as the go-to provider of sustainable materials for the food and beverage industry and in fashion, cosmetics and other consumer goods. In this scenario, Zerocircle expands its product line, continuously innovates and establishes strong partnerships with global brands committed to reducing their carbon footprint. Our success would be measured by the widespread adoption of our materials, our pivotal role in advancing the circular economy and the significant environmental impact we make on a global scale.

In another, equally promising future, Zerocircle can pivot and become a technology-driven enterprise, focusing on developing cutting-edge, sustainable, highly customizable and biodegradable materials for specific industrial needs. This path could involve advanced research and development, leading us to enter markets like biotechnology or advanced manufacturing, where our materials could be used in medical devices, electronics or other high-tech applications. In this scenario, Zerocircle would position itself at the forefront of technological innovation in sustainability. Its success would be marked by its ability to disrupt traditional industries and create entirely new markets. Both futures leverage our core strengths in materials innovation and reflect our commitment to sustainability.

Conclusion

Zerocircle is revolutionizing the fight against plastic pollution by repurposing one of nature's most abundant resources, seaweed, into an economically viable solution. More than a startup, it is a movement that challenges the status quo and offers a long-term solution to one of the world's most pressing environmental problems. As Zerocircle grows, it establishes a new benchmark for manufacturing truly eco-friendly materials, inspiring people to reassess how they interact with the earth and its resources. Its route exemplifies the impact that purpose-driven innovation can have on our environment.

13

How Battery Smart is Accelerating India's EV Movement

Imagine navigating through India's bustling streets, where the quiet, clean energy of EVs has replaced the hum of traditional engines. But behind this transformation would be a challenge that few had dared to tackle, one which makes EVs accessible and practical for everyone, from daily commuters to commercial drivers.

This is where Pulkit Khurana, Siddharth Sikka and Battery Smart emerge, driving a revolution to change how India moves.

Battery Smart solves a critical problem that has long hindered the rapid and large-scale adoption of EVs: the limitations of battery life and the inconvenience of long charging times. What caught our attention about Battery Smart when we first met Pulkit was the company's innovative approach to battery charging. Instead of drivers waiting for hours in a line to recharge their EV batteries at charging stations, they engage in battery swapping through Battery Smart's swapping partners, swap out a depleted battery for a fully charged one in minutes, making EVs more viable, especially in a country like India where time is a precious commodity and long waits can be frustrating and costly for daily wage earners. Pulkit had recognized early on that for EVs to truly take off, the infrastructure required to support them had to be as accessible as fuel stations for the traditional ICE-powered vehicles. This resulted in Battery Smart's partner-led model integrating battery swapping into existing local businesses.

The results are there for all to see: today, Battery Smart has 1,000 partner-led stations across thirty cities in India. This network has recently completed over 35 million swaps and continues to grow prolifically. Today, it is India's largest and fastest-growing battery-swapping network for electric two- and three-wheelers!

Pulkit Khurana and Siddharth Sikka's journey with Battery Smart is a powerful example of how innovative thinking can remove the barriers to sustainable change. Their work sets the stage for a cleaner, more efficient transportation system in India, proving that even the most daunting of challenges can be overcome with the right solutions. They are not just advocating for electric mobility but are making it a practical reality for millions in India.

1. How would you describe the climate problem your startup is solving in India?

India's transportation sector poses a major climate challenge because of its high carbon emissions. Driven by rapid economic growth and an expanding middle class, there has been a surge in vehicle usage, heavily reliant on diesel and petrol. This dependence on fossil fuels is a primary source of CO_2 emissions, which significantly contributes to global warming. Now it gets trickier. We've got a bunch of older, less efficient vehicles, particularly in congested urban areas, leading to higher emissions. The transportation infrastructure, characterized by traffic congestion and inadequate public transport, increases fuel consumption and emissions. This contributes to climate change and causes severe local air pollution, posing health risks in many Indian cities.

Efforts to shift towards sustainable transportation, like EVs and improved public transit, are in progress, but we still face obstacles such as high costs and insufficient infrastructure. The transport sector's heavy reliance on fossil fuels, coupled with outdated vehicles and infrastructure, is not just a global climate headache; it's causing serious havoc on the environment and our health in India.

2. Tell us a bit about yourselves. What was the spark that ignited your startup idea? Share with us that lightbulb moment.

Over the first few months of our journey which began in 2019, Siddharth and I travelled across various cities, talking to electric three-wheeler users. There were already over a million such drivers, making up more than 80 per cent of all EVs in India. During our visits to their homes and parking areas, we realized that these drivers' earning ability was limited because of the prohibitive battery costs and long charging times, and not because of poor demand for their service. This led us to think of better ways to improve their livelihood, which ultimately sparked the creation of Battery Smart.

3. Can you recall an 'Only in India' challenge you faced and the innovative way in which you tackled it?

Expanding battery-swapping stations across India posed a significant challenge for Battery Smart, primarily due to high real estate costs and diverse geographical conditions. The vastness of the country, coupled with its varied terrain, made establishment of a uniform network of stations, both complex and expensive. In urban areas, where the demand is high, real estate prices were also very high, making it financially burdensome to set up and maintain dedicated swapping stations. In rural and remote areas, logistical difficulties and lower demand added to the challenge.

To overcome these obstacles, we adopted a unique partner-led model. Instead of setting up standalone stations, we collaborated with existing local businesses, such as mom-and-pop shops and small stores. This approach offered us several advantages. First, it significantly reduced the overhead costs associated with acquiring and maintaining property, as these local businesses already had the necessary space and infrastructure. Second, it leveraged the widespread presence of these shops, ensuring a broader and more accessible network across diverse geographical regions, including harder-to-reach rural areas.

This innovation was key in enabling Battery Smart to swiftly grow its network across various regions (Battery Smart has already established swapping stations in Tier 1, 2 and 3 cities across several states in India including Haryana, Delhi-NCR, Karnataka, Rajasthan, Telangana, Uttar Pradesh and Maharashtra), ultimately becoming the largest battery-swapping network in the country.

4. Imagine your startup as a character from Indian mythology. Who would it be, and why?

If I were to imagine Battery Smart as a character from Indian mythology, it might be likened to Lord Hanuman from the Ramayana. Lord Hanuman is known for his strength, lightning speed, agility and relentless dedication to serving a higher cause. Similarly, the dense network of Battery Smart's battery-swapping stations and our two-minute battery swaps reflect the strength and speed of Lord Hanuman.

Lord Hanuman is also known for his problem-solving abilities and the ease with which he overcame obstacles. Similarly, Battery Smart aims to eliminate the major roadblocks in EV adoption, such as long charging downtimes, unreliable battery life, range anxiety (the fear or concern that a vehicle has insufficient battery charge to reach its destination, leading to worries about finding charging stations along the way) and high upfront costs. Our interoperable battery-swapping model can be seen as a clever and efficient solution to these challenges, aligning with Lord Hanuman's resourcefulness. The vision of having one swap station every square kilometre is ambitious and reflects the omnipresence and accessibility that Hanuman symbolizes in Indian mythology.

5. Which global company do you admire or draw inspiration from, and what aspects of its journey do you wish to emulate?

Battery Smart's commitment to providing financial empowerment and making electric mobility accessible for all commercial drivers mirrors Amazon's renowned philosophy of customer obsession. Just as Amazon revolutionized retail by prioritizing customer satisfaction and convenience, Battery Smart focuses on the specific needs of its driver community, aiming to transform its economic and operational experiences.

Central to Battery Smart's approach is the financial empowerment of drivers. Recognizing the economic challenges commercial drivers face, especially in transitioning to EVs, the company endeavours to make this shift both affordable and profitable. This is achieved by reducing the upfront costs of owning an EV and offering two-minute battery-swapping solutions. By lowering the barriers to entry for EV usage, Battery Smart ensures that drivers can seamlessly adopt this eco-friendly technology without financial strain.

Furthermore, Battery Smart simplifies the process of electric mobility, akin to how Amazon simplifies shopping. The accessibility and convenience of our battery-swapping stations ensure that drivers have easy and quick access to them for exchange of their depleted batteries with fully charged ones, significantly reducing downtime and increasing efficiency.

Battery Smart's driver-centric approach, focusing on affordability, accessibility and financial empowerment, resonates with Amazon's ethos of prioritizing customer needs. It demonstrates a deep commitment to revolutionizing the experience of its user base.

6. Paint us a picture of the opportunity landscape in India that your startup is tapping into. How big is this stage?

India currently has a staggering 350 million vehicles navigating its roads. What might surprise you is that a massive 77 per cent of this total, equivalent to 270 million, consists of two- and three-wheelers. Battery Smart has strategically set its sights on this specific market, aiming to empower and facilitate the transition of these vehicles to electric mobility.

7. If your startup journey was a Bollywood movie, what would be its title and who would you cast as yourself?

The title would be *Kabhi Rukna Nahi* (Never Stop). The movie would feature two lead actors. I would cast Amitabh Bachchan and Dharmendra – more like Jai and Veeru from *Sholay* – to play me and my co-founder Siddharth, respectively.

8. What myth about Indian climate startups would you bust with a fact or a story?

Many people believe that until the grid is 100 per cent renewable, EVs will not be making a massive environmental impact. However, that myth has been debunked in various research papers. There is a tangible CO_2 offset happening by eliminating tailpipe emissions. The grid in India is already 25 per cent green, with the goal being to reach 60 per cent within the decade. It is imperative to move towards EVs rapidly and en masse.

9. Describe a day in your life as a founder in India – the chaos, the calm and the caffeine.

As the founder of Battery Smart, my days are a dynamic mix of highs and lows. They typically involve a whirlwind of meetings and strategic decisions, of navigating the challenges of leading a nascent-stage startup. I invest significant time in forging collaborations with various stakeholders, including battery manufacturers, OEMs, drivers and fleet operators. This effort aims to create a unified platform that builds a comprehensive ecosystem, facilitating a seamless and economical transition to electric mobility for all the stakeholders involved.

The highlight lies in witnessing both the team and the company grow. Both celebrating successes and confronting failures create a strong sense of belonging and camaraderie among the team. In this startup journey, solving unique problems is the daily norm, and each challenge is viewed as an opportunity for innovation.

10. If you could have a cup of chai with an Indian (or global) environmental icon, who would it be and what would you ask?

I'd love to have a cup of chai with Elon Musk and ask him about the next frontier he sees but currently lacks the time to explore. I'd be curious to know how he sees that space evolving.

11. Which book, movie or figure in India has left a lasting mark on your entrepreneurial spirit?

Shawshank Redemption has always inspired me to appreciate the power of relentless effort and grit in achieving what seems impossible.

12. Fast-forward ten years – What's your vision of your startup's impact on India's climate action?

In a decade, Siddharth and I see Battery Smart playing a transformative role in India's transition to clean mobility, making electric vehicles accessible and affordable for all. A key part of this vision is reducing the initial cost of EVs, allowing a much broader segment of the population to adopt them.

Battery Smart aims to establish a battery-swapping station every square kilometre nationwide. This dense network will ensure that EV drivers are never far from a swapping station, effectively eliminating range anxiety and making electric mobility as convenient as traditional fuel-based options.

Our vision is to make ownership of an EV a stress-free and economical choice, free from concerns about charging times and maintenance. Battery Smart's future is one where electric mobility isn't just environmentally friendly, but also the most practical and economical choice for everyone.

13. Ever received feedback from an Indian customer that made you go 'Wow'? Tell us!

One of the most heartening pieces of feedback we received came from a driver whose experience with Battery Smart profoundly impacted her life. She expressed immense satisfaction with our services, particularly noting how the efficiency and cost-effectiveness of battery-swapping significantly boosted her earnings.

This positive change was so substantial that it led her to encourage her friends to leave their manufacturing jobs and join her in the e-rickshaw business. Her story is a testament to Battery Smart's solution's transformative potential, not just in terms of environmental impact but also in terms of economic empowerment of individuals.

14. Profit vs. planet – How does this debate shape your boardroom discussions?

At Battery Smart, the profit vs. planet debate is not a trade-off, but a symbiotic relationship between the two. We understand the responsibility of revolutionizing electric vehicle adoption in India and are committed to aligning our success with environmental sustainability.

Our partner-led approach, which involves collaborating with local businesses for rapid station deployment, is about more than just profitability – it's about using existing infrastructure wisely. This strategy minimizes the ecological footprint of building new infrastructure while ensuring business success.

Moreover, the additional income drivers generate using our battery-swapping services makes ownership of EVs financially attractive, encouraging more users to switch to EVs and accelerating the transition to clean mobility. We believe a successful and sustainable business model benefits the bottom line and the planet we all share.

15. When pitching to VCs, what's the core story or angle you use to captivate their interest in your startup? Share with us your narrative, especially in the context of India's unique climate challenges and opportunities.

Venture Capitalists recognize that transitioning to EVs is crucial in addressing climate change. However, they understand that adoption of EVs faces significant barriers, notably the high upfront costs and the challenges related to battery charging time and infrastructure. This is where battery swapping emerges as a key enabler, offering a practical solution to accelerate and make EV adoption more affordable.

Battery swapping technology addresses primary concerns, such as EV range anxiety and long charging times. Instead of waiting for hours for a vehicle to charge, drivers can quickly swap a depleted battery for a fully charged one, significantly reducing downtime. This convenience is particularly beneficial for commercial vehicles that cannot afford long charging breaks, making EVs more practical and appealing to a broader range of users.

Moreover, the battery-swapping model can potentially lower the initial cost of EVs. Since batteries are among the most expensive components of EVs, the ability to lease batteries separately from the vehicle can significantly reduce the upfront costs, making EVs financially accessible to more people.

With their strategic investments in battery-swapping technologies and related infrastructure, VCs are betting on this model as a catalyst for mass EV adoption. They understand that by mitigating key obstacles, battery swapping can be pivotal in India's transitioning to a more sustainable, electric-powered transportation system, aligning with global efforts to combat climate change.

16. For aspiring green entrepreneurs in India, what's your golden piece of advice?

For aspiring green entrepreneurs in India, my golden advice is to focus on building solutions that help the environment and deliver tangible value to customers. Addressing specific customer needs or problems is crucial, beyond just the environmental benefits. Whether it's cost savings, enhanced efficiency, better performance or improved health and safety, these added values can significantly elevate your offering's appeal.

Remember, the key to long-term success in the green sector is not just about being eco-friendly; it's about intertwining this with solutions that customers find practical, beneficial and valuable in their everyday lives. By achieving this balance, you foster customer loyalty and trust and open up new market opportunities, enhancing your brand's reputation and ensuring your business's sustainability in the ever-evolving market landscape.

17. If you could wave a magic wand, what one change would you bring to the Indian climate tech ecosystem?

If I could wave a magic wand, I would create a comprehensive and supportive environment for EV adoption in India. This vision would include robust government policies that promote EVs through financial incentives for consumers and manufacturers, alongside significant investments in sustainable technology R&D. It would also involve widespread infrastructure development, with battery-swapping stations becoming as common as traditional fuel stations, effectively addressing range anxiety and making EVs feasible even in remote areas. Additionally, enhancing public awareness and education would be crucial, the aim being to shift the mindset towards sustainability as a preferred choice and promoting a culture of environmental responsibility.

18. In your vision, what are two distinctly different but equally successful potential futures you see for your startup in the next five years?

In the next five years, Battery Smart envisions two potential paths for its future. In the first scenario, the company aims to establish an omnipresent battery-swapping network, empowering most electric vehicles across various form factors to access convenient, efficient and cost-effective battery-swapping services. This network would span every square kilometre of the top 100 cities, leading to an extensive network of strategically located battery-swapping stations, ensuring maximum convenience and accessibility for EV users. Battery Smart plans to partner with urban planners, city governments and mobility companies to integrate this swapping network into smart city initiatives and public transportation systems. Additionally, the company will focus on innovative technologies and process optimizations to reduce swapping times, increase network efficiency and enhance user experience, ultimately securing a dominant market position as the key enabler of rapid EV adoption.

In an alternative scenario, Battery Smart sees itself becoming the largest and most comprehensive battery-as-a-service platform, delivering integrated energy solutions for various mobility applications, renewable energy systems and grid-scale energy storage. This future would be characterized by a diversified portfolio of battery-swapping services for multiple electric vehicle types, including e-rickshaws, e-autos, e-buses and e-trucks. Strategic partnerships with renewable energy companies would allow Battery Smart to offer bundled energy storage solutions for solar, wind and other clean energy sources. The company would also develop advanced technology platforms to optimize battery performance, predict energy demand and enable seamless integration with various mobility and energy applications. Battery Smart would expand into new markets, including grid-scale energy storage, commercial and industrial energy solutions and residential energy storage, positioning itself as a leader in the clean energy landscape.

Conclusion

Battery Smart is quietly but effectively solving one of the biggest challenges in EV adoption – making charging of EVs hassle-free and fast. Its approach is refreshingly straightforward: swap out the battery and get back on the road. As Battery Smart grows, it's setting a new standard for what practical everyday electric mobility can and should look like in India – smart, simple and different!

14

Nutrifresh's Farm-to-Fork Hydroponics Journey

Revolutionizing the way the world grows its food requires a deep understanding of the land, the people and their challenges. Sanket Mehta and Ganesh Nikam's journey with Nutrifresh isn't just a startup story, but a bold reimagining of agriculture in India. What drew us to Nutrifresh's founders was not just their passion for sustainable farming but also their commitment to creating a system that could address the unique challenges of India's agricultural landscape. Nutrifresh offers a compelling example of how technology and tradition can come together to create something truly transformative.

Nutrifresh's founders didn't set out to grow food but to solve a problem that has long plagued Indian agriculture: the lack of consistency and quality in produce. Leveraging their backgrounds in finance and their deep connection to the land, Sanket and Ganesh turned to hydroponics – a method that allows crops to be grown in a controlled environment using

90 per cent less water than traditional farming – to ensure that the freshest, most nutritious produce reaches the consumer directly, eliminating intermediaries and reducing food miles.

Further, by employing 60 per cent of its workforce from women in nearby villages, this Pune-based startup provides livelihoods, empowers these communities and fosters in them a sense of ownership and pride in the produce they grow. This holistic approach to agriculture makes Nutrifresh a standout in the field.

Nutrifresh is paving the way for a new era of agriculture in India that is sustainable, scalable and deeply connected to the communities it serves. Sanket and his co-founder Ganesh are not just growing food but also nursing a vision for a more resilient and equitable future.

1. How would you describe the climate problem your startup is solving in India?

Nutrifresh started its operations in early 2019 after a thorough analysis of the crisis the world might face following a population explosion. It is estimated that the world will have 10 billion people to feed by 2050. The Stockholm International Water Institute states, 'There will not be enough water available on current croplands to produce food for the expected 10 billion population in 2050 if we follow current trends and changes towards diets common in Western nations.' This projection highlights the dual problems the world is facing: current croplands and water levels will be insufficient to feed the 10 billion people we will have on earth. Therefore, we need to pivot to alternative sources of food production and leverage technology to use our available resources more efficiently and effectively.

The Indian population, with an estimated 1.67 billion people, will form an integral part of this global challenge. At Nutrifresh, we are growing food most efficiently and sustainably using hydroponics, which is a method of growing fruits and vegetables in a controlled environment while using 90 per cent less water than traditional open-field farming. This method does not depend on fertile soil, making it possible to cultivate crops in areas that may be unsuitable for conventional farming. Thus, Nutrifresh addresses the dual challenges of enabling food production for future generations and nurturing a greener tomorrow.

2. Tell us a bit about yourselves. What was the spark that ignited your startup idea? Share with us that lightbulb moment.

After completing my master's in finance, I joined a public-sector bank as a scale-2 credit manager at a mid-corporate branch in Pune. I processed credit proposals, mainly from sectors like sugar, dairy, poultry, agriculture and ethanol, which required visiting various farms for assessments. I was astonished by the quality of the farm produce and milk at these locations. However, the same quality was not available back home in Mumbai, just 150 kilometres from Pune. Farmers faced additional challenges in selling their produce at good rates because they had to travel to mandis to understand the rates and were compelled to sell to agents at low prices because of the perishability of their produce.

Ganesh Nikam, my co-founder, had completed his MBA in finance and CFA level-3 from the USA and was running his own finance consultancy. He frequently visited the bank for various agri-credit proposals and became my go-to person for all my entry-level queries since he came from an agrarian family. After being bombarded with multiple queries, he offered his dad's help in answering them. We met over lunch and his dad said, 'If you really want to understand agriculture, get yourself dirty in the soil first, and then you will better understand the field.' This compelled us to experiment, leading to our lightbulb moment, and there has been no looking back since.

3. Can you recall an 'Only in India' challenge you faced and the innovative way you tackled it?

When we entered the hydroponics industry, we understood that there were few vendors in the Indian market, and most of the equipment, the non-GMO seeds and fertilizers for it were imported. We were amazed that while the Indian economy is 70 per cent dominated by agriculture, we still import most of the inputs. However, we wanted to be recognized as an Indian brand, so we tried to indigenize whatever we could. We handpicked various vendors who were ready to innovate. We contacted multiple importers of agricultural equipment, visited factories and indigenized the ideas we saw, reverse-engineering them to suit our geographical requirements in India. This is how we managed the 'Only in India' challenge.

4. Imagine your startup as a character from Indian mythology. Who would it be, and why?

I consider my startup as similar to Chanakya from Indian mythology. I admire Chanakya for the design of his strategies in his work, the *Arthashastra*, which discusses one of my favorite subjects, economic policy. The best thing about business is not being at the top and making all the decisions, but creating leaders capable of making the right decisions and working as a team for the company, making irreversible changes that solve real problems.

5. Which global company do you admire or draw inspiration from, and what aspects of its journey do you wish to emulate?

I personally admire UAE's Pure Harvest and China's Le Gaga Holdings' journeys; they operate in the same sector. The best part of Pure Harvest's journey is that the company understood the challenge it was confronted with and grabbed the best opportunity with minimum resources. Pure Harvest's growth is purpose-driven, which fuels its upward journey. Le Gaga Holdings has a model that is similar to Nutrifresh's and has witnessed quick growth with stable financials. We want to emulate the best of both worlds.

6. Paint us a picture of the opportunity landscape in India that your startup is tapping into. How big is this stage?

Nutrifresh is solving the major problem of inconsistency in the fruits and vegetables one gets in India through the seasons and addresses the nutritional quality of the produce. Even today, greens like spinach are grown near railway tracks in India using untreated water. The market for our produce is huge, since we are dealing in daily consumables and promising consistency in quality, residue-free produce, high nutrition and affordability. Every household in tier-1 to tier-3 cities in India is potentially our customer.

7. If your startup journey was a Bollywood movie, what would be its title and who would you cast as yourself?

If Nutrifresh were a Bollywood film, *Paisa Kamaya Nahi, Banaya Jata Hai* would be the title of its startup journey. Allu Arjun would play me – a driven, impetuous and aggressive person ready to tackle any chore and finish it. Vikrant Massey would portray Ganesh, my co-founder, as a cool, collected, driven and calm entrepreneur in charge of guiding the business. Both approaches are absolutely necessary to keep the company in balance.

8. What myth about Indian climate startups would you bust with a fact or a story?

Most climate startups must identify the problem and then find multiple solutions to it, selecting the most sustainable option. However, it often works the other way around. Many climate startups in India have a solution and try to fit it to solve a climate problem. One such incident happened with us when some Dutch companies pitched their glasshouse structures for our farm set-up in India. They emphasized the climate benefits of glasshouses over the traditional poly-houses, but glasshouses are ten times more expensive and not economically viable for us.

9. Describe a day in your life as a founder in India – the chaos, the calm and the caffeine.

Initially, when we started Nutrifresh, everything was chaotic. From defining the unit of measurement for each category of products, billing, accounting, agronomy, tech and people management, we wore all the hats. We even drove tempos to delivery locations and delivered our veggies ourselves. Now, with a great team and the best talent in the industry, our management is solid. We allocate our time to business building, evaluating new ideas, reviewing financials and acting as a fire brigade wherever the team needs help to perform better.

10. If you could have a cup of chai with an Indian (or global) environmental icon, who would it be and what would you ask him or her?

I would really have loved to meet Ratan Tata. He was a visionary who has shown that no matter how difficult situations can get, patience and determination lead to success. I would have asked him how to create meaningful businesses.

11. Which book, movie or figure in India has left a lasting mark on your entrepreneurial spirit?

I am a great Bollywood fan, and the one movie I love to watch again and again is *83 – World Cup*. Although it may not be directly related to entrepreneurial spirit, Kapil Dev's statement at a press conference – 'We are here to win' – and the memorable six he hit into the dressing room during a challenging moment to boost the Indian team's confidence made a lasting impression on me.

12. Fast-forward ten years – What's your vision of your startup's impact on India's climate action?

In the next ten years, I would love to see more fresh water available for daily purposes, and green forests and nutritious vegetables available for all.

13. Ever received feedback from an Indian customer that made you go 'Wow'? Tell us!

I was travelling from Mumbai to Delhi and waiting in the security queue at the airport one day with a box of Nutrifresh produce. An elderly couple near me started whispering to each other when they noticed it. The lady asked, 'Do you also buy veggies from Nutrifresh?' I replied, 'Yes.' She asked, 'Do they deliver at the airport too?' I said, 'No, I ordered these directly from Nutrifresh.' She responded, 'Ahh, I really love the spinach and cherry tomatoes. You should also try lemon grass and Lollo lettuce. The baby spinach and kale are out of this world. I didn't like the celery much; it needs to be sturdier, but the parsley is amazing. Basil is something I really recommend.'

I smiled and nodded. After the security check, I met them and explained that I was the founder of Nutrifresh. It was a pleasure to hear first-hand, unbiased opinions of our produce.

14. Profit vs. planet – How does this debate shape your boardroom discussions?

Our approach is balanced. We take the middle ground to make irreversible changes and ensure the longevity of food security. We weigh each change against its economic viability and make decisions based on the scale at which such changes make financial sense for the company. This approach drives us to achieve scale-oriented goals in a staggered manner. Even in our boardroom discussions, this approach guides us.

15. When pitching to VCs, what's the core story or angle you use to captivate their interest in your startup? Share with us your narrative, especially from the perspective of India's unique climate challenges and opportunities.

The key points of our pitch that grab investor attention are our 90 per cent water consumption cut from open-field farming, creative use of barren terrain to grow several crops in poly houses and our dedication to empowering local communities by hiring 60% women from surrounding villages. Furthermore, investors relate to our position as a profit-making, sustainable company. These elements, taken together, showcase not only our present achievement but also the exciting future possibilities of our path.

16. For aspiring green entrepreneurs in India, what's your golden piece of advice?

I want to narrate a line from a song, '*Ruk jana nahin tu kahin haar ke, kaanton pe chalke milenge saaye bahaar ke, O raahi, O raahi . . .*', which translates into English as 'Don't stop anywhere in defeat, by walking on thorns you will find the shadows of spring, O traveller, O traveller.' This line from a famous Bollywood song carries a message of perseverance and resilience. It encourages the listener, referred to as 'raahi' (traveller), to keep moving forward despite the challenges and difficulties (symbolized by 'thorns') along the way. The idea is that even though your path may be tough, if you keep going you will eventually reach a place of beauty and success ('shadows of spring'). The song serves as a reminder that giving up is not an option and that the enduring of hardships will lead to better days.

17. If you could wave a magic wand, what one change would you bring to the Indian climate tech ecosystem?

I don't believe in magic – only in effort, determination and a little luck.

18. In your vision, what are two distinctly different but equally successful potential futures you see for your startup in the next five years?

One is that we are the biggest growers of fruits and vegetables in a controlled environment across Asia; the other is that we have the largest network of farmers growing fruits and vegetables in a controlled environment, making us the biggest manufacturers of processed foods in Asia.

Conclusion

Nutrifresh is not just a controlled-environment agriculture business. It's a new way of thinking about how we ought to grow and deliver our food! Sanket and Ganesh's commitment to climate change and their combined vision for a direct farm-to-fork connection have made Nutrifresh a category leader in its line of business in India. With the right blend of technology and community focus, Nutrifresh is proving daily that real change starts with a single seed. With commitment and nurturing, we can build a better food system for people and the planet.

Afterword

India is currently in the midst of a startup revolution that is shaking up our fossil fuel based economy and accelerating India's green future. Picture a high-energy Bollywood dance number – only, instead of dazzling choreography, we are talking about electric vehicles, plant-based dairy and tech innovations. Companies like RevFin, ElectricPe, Accacia, Batterysmart, BluSmart Mobility, Nutrifresh, CHUPPS, Zero Cow, Log9 Materials, EMotorad and NeoCell Industries are leading the charge, and they are doing it with flair.

These companies have much in common: (1) they are mission-driven around a deep purpose; (2) they have understood India's unique challenges; (3) they are using technology in truly innovative ways; (4) they have been able to forge a win-win ecosystem around their solutions; and (5) they are finding unique approaches to scaling rapidly so that they can keep attracting customers and investors. These distinctive attributes have catapulted them to the front of the pack in India's burgeoning green startup ecosystem.

Deep Purpose

India's journey towards a greener future isn't just about making money – it's also driven by a deeper sense of purpose. The idea of 'deep purpose', as introduced by Professor Ranjay Gulati at Harvard Business School, is about finding the 'why' that drives a business, beyond just the making of money. It's about aligning profits with a positivc impact on socicty, and these companies are nailing it. Take Nutrifresh, for instance. Founders Sanket Mehta and Ganesh Nikam didn't just want to grow vegetables; they wanted to revolutionize Indian agriculture. They saw the problems of inconsistent produce quality and water scarcity and thought, 'Why not farm without soil and use 90 per cent less water while we're at it?' Their hydroponic farming model not only improves yields but also empowers local women by providing them with jobs. It is purpose with a punch of practicality.

BluSmart's founders, Punit Goyal and Anmol Jaggi, also embrace deep purpose. Tired of breathing the city smog and watching fuel prices soar, they decided to create a ride-hailing service that doesn't just get you from point A to B, but does so with zero emissions. BluSmart's mission is to 'decarbonize mobility at scale', and the founders make this happen with a fleet of shiny electric cars that don't leave behind any tailpipe fumes. BluSmart is a ride-hailing service that's clean, green and a little bit mean (towards pollution, that is).

Zero Cow Factory's founders Sohil and Parini Kapadia are on a mission to disrupt India's dairy industry without involving a single cow. Think of them as the unlikely superheroes of dairy, using precision fermentation to create animal-free dairy proteins. Their motivation? To cut the massive environmental impact of traditional dairy farming, which involves millions of methane-belching cows. They're not just making milk; they're reimagining an entire industry and, in the process, proving that you don't need an animal with four stomachs to make cheese.

Log9 Materials, led by Akshay Singhal, is driven by a deep-seated purpose to make EVs work better in India's challenging climate. Akshay's fascination with graphene and the company's battery innovation are more than tech obsessions; they are about solving a real problem – how to make batteries that can withstand India's sweltering heat and chaotic usage patterns. The company's purpose is more than just the electrifying of vehicles; it's about powering a cleaner future, one charge at a time.

This sense of deep purpose that drives these companies also leads to highly engaged employees, deep-rooted partnerships and committed investors. It is also the best pathway to getting beyond just profits, to actually build great, enduring companies. These companies are special not just in what they are doing, but also in how they are doing it.

Solving India's Problems

India has its own set of unique business challenges, and these companies aren't afraid to roll up their sleeves and come up with solutions that work for everyone in India. CHUPPS, for example, took one look at the billions of shoes piling up in landfills in India and decided it was time for a makeover – one that's fashionable and biodegradable. With footwear that breaks down in just over a year, CHUPPS is making a statement: You can be eco-friendly without sacrificing style. It's a step in the right direction – literally.

Battery Smart saw a different kind of problem: the dreaded EV charging wait for autorickshaw drivers that would take them off the road and stop them from earning their daily wages. We've all been there, watching the clock tick as the battery stubbornly and slowly fills up, but this is really painful for those who earn their living from driving people around. Battery Smart's solution? A swapping system that lets you switch out a dead battery for a fresh one faster than you can say 'back on the road'. It's quick, convenient and keeps the wheels turning for autorickshaw drivers.

NeoCell Industries is tackling an even bigger challenge: fossil fuel dependence. With their cutting-edge lithium battery technology, NeoCell is helping reduce emissions from India's two- and three-wheelers, turning the country's roads into less of a smog parade. Their high-energy-density cells are not just powering vehicles but also powering change, proving that even the smallest tech upgrades can have a massive impact.

India's challenges are as diverse as its cuisines, but these companies are taking them head on with innovative solutions. For RevFin, it's about making electric vehicles accessible to those at the bottom of the financial pyramid who do not have access to loans from typical lenders. Autorickshaw drivers, gig economy drivers and other people employed in the informal sector have not established a credit history and generally do not own any property that can be used as security for a loan. Founder Sameer Aggarwal's finance background gave him a front-row seat from which he could view the struggles of the underserved, and now, through RevFin, he's financing EVs for those who never thought they'd own one. Imagine switching from a rickety old diesel three-wheeler to a sleek, quiet e-rickshaw; it's not just about going green, it's about economic empowerment with a green twist.

Meanwhile, Accacia is tackling the giant carbon footprint of India's real estate sector. Founder Annu Talreja didn't start with dreams of entrepreneurship; it took a close encounter with flash floods in Indonesia for her to realize the urgent need for change in the construction industry. With Accacia, she's helping companies track and reduce their emissions, making the real estate sector part of the climate solution rather than just another problem. Think of it as giving buildings a smart tracker – except, instead of counting steps it's counting CO_2 emissions.

EMotorad, led by Adi Oza and his team of friends-turned-founders, takes on India's transportation woes with electric bikes. With cities choked by traffic and air pollution, EMotorad's e-bikes are a breath of fresh air. By creating stylish, affordable e-bikes, they're not just selling a product; they're fostering a culture of sustainable commuting. It's like trading your stressful car commute for a bike ride that's good for both your health and the planet.

Use of Sophisticated Technologies

Innovation is about creating solutions that make life better, and these companies are on it. Nutrifresh's hydroponic systems are a prime example. No soil? No problem. Their tech allows crops to flourish in controlled environments, producing high-quality food all year round. It's farming that's straight out of the future. Log9 Materials is pioneering battery technology that's specifically tailored to meet India's tough conditions. Their advanced battery chemistry, which improves thermal resilience and reduces charge times, isn't just high tech; it's high stakes. By making batteries that last longer and charge faster, they're tackling the 'India problem' of EVs, making them reliable in a climate where summer isn't just hot but blistering.

BluSmart's tech game is strong, too. Their all-electric fleet isn't just about being green – it's about creating a seamless user experience with tech that optimizes routes, manages energy and keeps the whole operation running smoothly.

NeoCell's batteries are basically the overachievers of the battery world. Their Silicon Nickel Manganese Cobalt (NMC) cells offer better range, faster charging and improved safety – all while keeping the environmental impact low. It's a tech upgrade that's doing more than just powering cars; it's powering India's green future. Sophisticated technology is at the heart of these companies' solutions, turning big ideas into practical impacts. Zero Cow Factory uses precision fermentation – a process that's more like brewing beer than farming. By fermenting microbes to produce dairy proteins, they've taken a centuries-old practice and turned it into a futuristic, sustainable alternative to conventional dairy.

RevFin's innovation lies not just in the e-vehicles but also in their financing model. By using behavioural data instead of traditional credit scores, the company has cracked the code to making finance accessible to underserved communities. EMotorad's e-bikes are built with tech that blends style and function. From their removable batteries to their sleek design, their bikes are pushing technology to the utmost for the Indian bike enthusiast. EMotorad has also innovated in their factory design, so that their bikes can be made efficiently and quickly. Technology is woven into all their business operations, and they keep improving on every dimension continuously.

Ecosystem Management

Running a sustainable business is about managing the whole ecosystem to solve customer problems. Nutrifresh, for instance, integrates local communities into its operations, creating a closed-loop system where everyone benefits. By cutting out the middlemen and employing local women, Nutrifresh is growing opportunity across the ecosystem. NeoCell's focus on supply chain management is a masterstroke. By developing a domestic supply chain for their lithium cells, they're cutting down on imports, supporting local industries and making their operations more sustainable. Similarly, RevFin is knitting together the finance and EV ecosystems, partnering with OEMs, dealers and providers of charging infrastructure.

Log9 Materials is creating a network of partners, from EV manufacturers to fleet operators, to ensure their batteries are used effectively across the market. Accacia is connecting the dots in the real estate sector, bringing together building owners, vendors and green finance. Their ecosystem approach makes it easier for businesses to adopt sustainable practices without having to navigate a maze of disconnected solutions.

Battery Smart's ecosystem management is also about partnerships. Instead of building their own costly stations, they've teamed up with local businesses, turning everyday shops into battery-swapping hubs. It's a win-win system that keeps costs down and accessibility up, proving that sometimes the best solutions come from entities working together. Managing a complex ecosystem is crucial for scaling sustainable solutions. Zero Cow Factory is building a new dairy ecosystem without cows, tapping into India's strength in biotech and low-cost manufacturing to scale their operations. They're creating an entire value chain, from lab to market, and proving that India can lead in this cutting-edge space.

BluSmart's ecosystem approach means they don't just focus on cars; they look at the bigger picture, including the charging infrastructure and energy partnerships that make the whole system work. It's like a perfectly choreographed dance between vehicles, power grids and tech, all working together to make urban mobility cleaner and more efficient. To that end, they have forged partnerships with car manufacturers to get EVs delivered to them quickly, and with green power suppliers so that their cars are charged using green energy wherever possible. EMotorad's ecosystem is all about accessibility – whether it's through government partnerships that lower costs or by ensuring their bikes are available in both urban and rural areas.

Rapid Scaling

Green scaling isn't just about growth; it's about growing with purpose. The faster these companies can scale, the greater the impact they will have. For instance, in the dairy world, Zero Cow Factory is completely flipping the narrative. While most startups are trying to innovate within the system, Sohil Kapadia is busy redefining the system itself, by producing dairy without cows. To grow fast, Zero Cow does not need cows, but factories full of fermentation vats. As Sohil points out, the dairy industry is one of the largest contributors to greenhouse gas emissions, with each cow producing up to 500 litres of methane daily. By removing cows from the equation, his company has figured out how to satisfy dairy lovers while dramatically cutting down environmental damage.

BluSmart's all-in-one model has enabled it to expand rapidly in a fiercely competitive market. By owning every part of the process – from the EV cars to the charging stations –

they've built a business that's as scalable as it is sustainable. The more cars they can put on the road, the faster they can help India reduce its emissions. NeoCell's rapid scaling is backed by booming demand and government support, positioning them as a key player in India's transition to electric mobility. With every new battery they produce, NeoCell is powering a nationwide movement towards a greener, more sustainable future.

Akshay Singhal and the team at Log9 Materials understood that India's tropical climate required very different battery chemistries for scaling rapidly. In India's soaring heat, typical lithium-ion batteries can see their performance and lifespan plummet. Log9 Materials is pioneering high-temperature-resilient batteries that not only last longer but charge faster too. It's no surprise they're growing rapidly. Who wouldn't want a battery that survives the heat, lasts longer and powers their EVs for endless delivery runs? Log9 Materials's innovations mean fewer emissions and more uptime for electric vehicles, which means they're becoming the poster child of India's commercial electric mobility push.

Battery Smart's partner-led model lets them scale at warp speed, setting up new swapping stations faster than you can say 'climate action'. With over 1,000 stations across 30 cities, they're making EV adoption more feasible for thousands of autorickshaw drivers every month. And CHUPPS is not just about footwear. They've turned the entire Indian footwear market upside down with their biodegradable sliders, which can be disposed of without overburdening landfills. So every pair that they sell is a pair that is saving our environment.

Nutrifresh's hydroponic model of cultivating produce is built for replication, allowing the company to expand quickly without sacrificing quality or sustainability. They've turned the farm-to-fork concept into a finely tuned machine, connecting growers and consumers in a way that's efficient, transparent and green. Finally, there is EMotorad, which is gearing up to lead the green commute revolution, one electric bike at a time. If you've seen someone pedalling their way to work on a sleek, electric two-wheeler, you've probably spotted an EMotorad. The company is zooming, having sold over 1,00,000 e-bikes in a market that was once dominated by fossil-fuel-powered vehicles. What's their scaling secret? Simple: good, old-fashioned affordability mixed with government-backed incentives and snazzy designs. After all, if you're going to ride an electric bike, why not do it in style? EMotorad isn't just aiming for Indian streets either – they've got their eyes set on the global market, making their ride one to watch out for.

Green scaling is a special process. When these companies figure out what is required to grow quickly – whether it is fermentation vats for Zero Cow, land for Nutrifresh, BluSmart's electric vehicles or autorickshaw batteries for Battery Smart – they bet the company on acquiring more of this scarce resource. This then drives their growth, in a way that is very difficult for others to replicate. They are building sustainable competitive advantage by acquiring these scaling resources. But there is more. Every time they sell their products or services to their customers, they actually reduce India's greenhouse gas emissions. Combating climate change is both profitable and meaningful for them.

The Future We Want

As India continues its journey of growth and transformation, the contributions of these innovative startups highlight the potential of creativity and entrepreneurship in dealing with society's most difficult problems. These companies are proving that with the right mix of purpose, technology and collaboration, it's possible to make a real difference in the country.

These green entrepreneurs are driving India's growth and combating global climate change. The companies featured in this book have already created thousands of jobs and positively impacted crores of lives. They have saved millions of tons of carbon from entering the environment. In important ways, they are shaping our collective future. Such mission-driven entrepreneurs, their companies and the green companies that will follow them, may make the difference between sustainable prosperity and strife-ridden poverty for India. Most importantly, with their mix of innovation, impact and the joy they create for all, these companies show that transforming the world doesn't have to be dull. In fact, it can be the most exciting journey of all.

Acknowledgements

India's Green Startups would not have been possible without the guidance and inspiration of some key thought leaders. We extend our deepest gratitude to Nandan Nilekani, Amitabh Kant, Rajat Gupta, Nick Stern, Amar Bhattacharya, Martin Wolf, Sunjay Kapoor, Saurabh Srivastava, Ravi Venkatesan, Ranjay Gulati and Tarun Khanna for their invaluable insights and encouragement. Their perspectives shaped and refined the framework of our narrative and strengthened its purpose.

We are immensely thankful to the founders of the startups featured in this book. Every journey was unique, filled with challenges, breakthroughs and moments of profound learning. Your willingness to share your stories openly, engage deeply and patiently respond to continuous requests has not only enriched this book but also inspired us personally. Your vision and determination are a testament to the entrepreneurial spirit driving meaningful change in India.

A heartfelt thanks to the team at Green Frontier Capital, one of India's leading climate-tech venture capital firms based in Mumbai. Green Frontier Capital's meticulous tracking of hundreds of companies and exceptional data analysis made the selection process for the profiled ventures both rigorous and rewarding.

Special appreciation goes to Rhea Bhammer, Ritika Jajoo and Arjun Sinha for their invaluable feedback on the manuscript. Their thoughtful suggestions enhanced the clarity of our work and made it more engaging for a younger audience. Many thanks to Chiki Sarkar, Swati Chopra and their team at Juggernaut Books for their outstanding editorial support and keen guidance.

Finally, we take full responsibility for any errors or omissions in this book, which are entirely our own.

A Note on the Authors

Jayant Sinha is a distinguished Indian policymaker and investor, having chaired the Finance Committee in Parliament (2019–2024) and served as Minister of State for Finance and Civil Aviation (2014–2019). His policy achievements include developing India's bankruptcy code, architecting the tax code for Alternative Investment Funds, establishing India's National Investment and Infrastructure Fund and Higher Education Financing Agency, launching the UDAN and DigiYatra schemes and helping privatize Air India. Sinha has also led many climate policy initiatives, such as introducing India's first net zero bill in Parliament. As a venture capitalist, he has three unicorns to his credit and is widely recognized as one of the key shapers of India's startup ecosystem. Previously, he held leadership roles at Omidyar Network and McKinsey & Company. Sinha holds degrees from IIT Delhi, the University of Pennsylvania and Harvard Business School.

Sandiip Bhammer is the founder and managing partner of Green Frontier Capital, a leading India-focused climate-tech venture firm. With over 30 years of global finance experience, he has held prominent investment roles at DA Capital, Balyasny Asset Management and the Amaranth Group, as well as senior investment banking positions at Citigroup, HSBC and CLSA. As an adjunct professor of Finance at UMass Amherst's Isenberg School of Management he taught sustainability-focused startup investing. He continues to mentor and serve on several startup boards across India and the USA. Sandiip holds an MBA from Cornell University's Johnson Graduate School of Management, an MSc in Finance and a BSc in Business Administration from Boston College's Carroll School of Management. He was awarded the 2022 Meaningful Business 100 Award.